TRUE TO LIFE

ENGLISH FOR ADULT LEARNERS

PRE-INTERMEDIATE

Ruth Gairns
Stuart Redman

PERSONAL STUDY
WORKBOOK

Published by the Press Syndicate of the University of Cambridge
The Pitt Building, Trumpington Street, Cambridge CB2 1RP
40 West 20th Street, New York, NY 10011–4211, USA
10 Stamford Road, Oakleigh, Melbourne 3166, Australia

© Cambridge University Press 1995

First published 1995

Printed in Great Britain
at the University Press, Cambridge

ISBN 0 521 42146 2 Personal Study Book 2
ISBN 0 521 42145 4 Classbook 2
ISBN 0 521 42147 0 Teacher's Book 2
ISBN 0 521 42148 9 Class Cassette Set 2
ISBN 0 521 42149 7 Personal Study Cassette Set 2

CONTENTS

GETTING STARTED

We use the present continuous to talk about things happening now at this moment, and temporary things happening around now, but not necessarily at this moment.

Look at the groups of sentences. Put them in order from the shortest activity to the longest activity.

Example: *I'm writing a play.* **c = longest**
                    a shopping list. **a = shortest**
                    a letter to my brother. **b = in the middle**

Now you continue.

1. She's studying	a text from her coursebook. German. the map.	4. He's doing	his homework. a university degree in law. a typing course.
2. He's looking for	a new job. a present for his sister. his glasses.	5. She's reading	a novel by Tolstoy. an article in the paper. a notice.
3. She's working on	an advertising project. a new drug. an essay for tomorrow.	6. He's making	a movie. a sandwich. a pair of trousers.

Read the texts and underline the correct answers.

1. I (*come / am coming*) from Sweden, but I (*live / am living*) in Cambridge at the moment, because I (*do / am doing*) an English course at a language school. I (*stay / am staying*) with an English family who (*live / are living*) just outside the city centre. I (*work / am working*) for a large company which (*makes / is making*) sports equipment.

2. I (*save up / am saving up*) to do a language course in the United States next year because I (*work / am working*) in advertising, and almost everyone in this business (*speaks / is speaking*) English. At the moment I (*do / am doing*) an evening course, just three hours a week, but I've got an American friend who I (*meet / am meeting*) regularly, and we always (*speak / are speaking*) English to each other.

Now write a short text about yourself, similar to one of the texts above. If you like, give it to your teacher to check.

....

....

....

....

3 There's a mistake – it should be ...

use of *should*

Two learners wrote about their desks. We have underlined their mistakes. Correct them like this, using *should*:

Example: *'in my desk'* **should be** *'on my desk'*.

1.
My desk
My desk in Treviso is generally very organised and tidy. I like to have everything in order! <u>In my desk</u>, on the left, there is a <u>lamp table</u>. On the right there is a case for my letters. It was a <u>birthday's</u> present.

I like it because it is very bright! On the right there is also a plant. <u>Some times</u> there are books and pens, but generally I don't like to have <u>too much</u> things <u>in my desk</u>.

Chiara

2.
My desk
My desk is very nice. <u>His</u> big and I have a lot of stuff on it. I'm a bit untidy but I know where everything is. The important <u>think</u> for me is my notepads; I have four <u>in my right</u> because I <u>write always</u> many things. I have a big ruler, <u>two dictionary</u> – one English, one Greek. Of course I have a cup for my coffee or water because I drink <u>a lot water</u>.

Maria

4 On my desk

writing

Write a short text about your own desk or workplace, similar to the ones above. Look again at the texts on page 8 of the Class Book before you begin.

....

....

....

....

The instructions in this book may use some words that you don't know. This exercise will help you.

A Find examples of these in the box.

a sentence   a full stop   a hyphen   a comma   a phrase

a question mark   a capital letter

on the way   (prefer)   Where?
✗   'I don't like it,' he said.
it's   well-paid   condition   ✓   hospital

a tick   an apostrophe

a cross   word stress   brackets

B Underline a word in each sentence below which has a synonym in the box, and write the synonym in the space at the end of the line.

right   error   leave out   fill in   incorrect   select   understanding
not true   written description

Can you find the mistake? ...*error*............

You can identify any problems of comprehension. ....

As they talk about the pictures, complete the table below. ....

The words below are in the wrong order. ....

Keep a record of new vocabulary. ....

Decide which story is false. ....

Choose the best answer. ....

You can omit the second question. ....

Are these answers correct? ....

▭▭ The text below is adapted from the beginning of *Dark Angel*, by Sally Beauman. There are a lot of mistakes in it. Listen to the recording and follow the instructions.

I went to a fortune teller once His name was Mr Chaterjee; he had a small shop between a pastry-maker's and a silk-dealer, (in the middle of the bazaar), in Delhi.
It was not my idea to consult Mr Chat   . I did not believe in fortune-tellers, horoscopes, tarot cards or any of that kind of thing. Nor did my friend Wexton, but he was always full of surprises and when he suggested that I go, I thought: *Why not*
'Won't you also come too Wexton?' I said. 'He could read both our fortunes.' Wexton smiled. 'At my age,' he replied, 'you don t need a fortune-teller to predict your future, Victoria.'

Now check your corrected text with the text on page 140.

A Read about two more famous writers and complete each text with words from the box.

copy	antique	before	calendar	early	routine	type	diary
ugly	by hand	get up	previous				

Russell Hoban

I usually .... at about eight thirty or nine o'clock, and after breakfast I come to my desk. I suppose I am a creature of habit because I have a very strict .... First, I cross off yesterday on the ...., then I write in my .... what I did yesterday. After that, I select my music for the day, and I make a .... of what I wrote the day .... on my word processor.

Jessie Kesson

I bought an .... armchair and I sit there every day to write. I need cigarettes and lots of cups of tea or coffee. Some days, I get up as .... as four thirty; that gives me time to think. I go back and read what I wrote the .... day. My pencil is almost part of myself – I write everything .... I can't ...., and in any case, I certainly couldn't write straight onto a typewriter. I couldn't think of the words. Words are .... things and hard to work with.

B Look at the texts about Jeffrey Archer and Sally Beauman again in your Class Book, and answer the following questions, which are about all *four* writers.

1. Who smokes?
2. Who works on a typewriter?
3. Who writes in a diary every day?
4. Who gets up earliest?
5. Who likes to work with background music?
6. Who likes to work in a mess?
7. Who is the tidiest?
8. Who is the most like you?

8 Speaking partners

This is your first meeting, so begin with something easy to talk about in English. Here are four ideas:

1. Compare your answers to the visual dictionary exercise below, and any other exercises from Unit 1.

2. Tell your partner what you usually do in your free time. Do you have similar interests? Which?

3. Did you write anything in Reflections? If so, discuss it with your partner.

4. What do you find easy and difficult about learning English?

Before you finish, make sure you arrange another meeting together.

9 Visual dictionary

Label the pictures on page 119. Use a bilingual dictionary to help you.

10 Reflections

This space is for you to make a note of things you have learnt in this unit. You can also use it as a diary to write about your problems and progress in English.

....

....

....

....

....

....

....

....

....

....

....

....

....

....

ASKING QUESTIONS

1 Jumbled questions

Here are some questions from Unit 2 of the Class Book. Put the words in the correct order.

1. grow   she   where   up   did   ?
2. don't   why   you   them   visit   ?
3. well-paid   people   profession   your   are   in   ?
4. for   do   vote   who   you   ?
5. the   know   do   is   station   where   you   ?
6. flat   is   what   your   like   ?
7. spend   how   do   much   month   you   each   ?
8. building   is   what   it   of   type   ?
9. politics   you   in   are   interested   ?
10. do   how   earn   you   much   ?

2 What, where and how often?

A Complete the dialogue using question words from the box.

How	Where	How long	Whose	How far	What	Why
How often	When	Which				

1. A: .... do you live?   B: In Naples.

2. A: .... did you arrive?   B: A few days ago.

3. A: .... did you get here?   B: By car.

4. A: .... car is it? Yours?   B: No, it belongs to my uncle.

5. A: .... way did you come?   B: Through Milan and Paris.

6. A: .... is it?   B: I don't know. Over 1,000 miles.

7. A: .... did it take?   B: About twenty-four hours.

8. A: .... was the journey like?   B: Terrible!

9. A: .... do you come here?   B: Once or twice a year.

10. A: .... don't you go by plane?   B: Because I'm frightened of flying.

B Answer these questions about a good friend.

1. When did you first meet him/her?
2. Where did you meet him/her?
3. How did you meet him/her?
4. What does he/she do?
5. How old is he/she?
6. What are his/her hobbies?
7. What is he/she like?
8. How far is his/her home from yours?
9. How often do you see him/her?
10. Why do you like him/her?

Next time you see your speaking partner, tell them your answers.

3 Opposites and contrasts

The word *whereas* is used when we want to express a difference between *two subjects*.

Examples: **Mark** is tall whereas **Paul** is short.
In **the west** there are lots of mountains whereas **the east** is very flat.

Now complete the following sentences with a suitable word. If you don't know the word in English, use your first language and then a bilingual dictionary to help you.

1. John did well at school whereas I did .... most of the time.

2. He worked quite hard whereas I was very ....

3. He passed all his exams whereas I .... most of mine.

4. I always found exams difficult whereas he found them ....

5. He found lessons interesting whereas I thought they were ....

6. I left at sixteen whereas he .... at school until he was eighteen.

7. He really enjoyed school whereas I .... it.

8. Now he has a good job whereas I'm ....

Keep a record of words and phrases which form opposites.

Examples: *do well*   opposite = *do badly*
pass an exam   opposite = *fail an exam*

4 Catch the pronoun

It can be difficult to hear pronouns (e.g. *his/her; him/her*) because we sometimes 'eat' our words and join them together.

▭ Listen and write down the eight sentences. Some of them are the same as those in Exercise 2, Part B, but not all of them, so be careful. And sometimes the speaker uses *him*, sometimes *her* and sometimes *them*.

5 Stress and rhythm

▭ Listen to the sentences from Exercise 4 again and mark the stressed syllables on the key words as in the examples:

Examples: *When did you first meet him?*
Where did you meet her?

Do the same for all the sentences. Then, listen to the recording again and practise by repeating first the key words, then the whole sentences.

6 Kangaroos

A Use your dictionary to find the meaning of these words and write a translation or explanation next to each one. Remember that the topic is kangaroos.

a pouch ....

to hop ....

to jump ....

upright ....

to feed on something ....

an enemy ....

a species ....

B What would you like to know about kangaroos? Write down ten questions.

Examples: *How long do they live?*
Why are they called kangaroos?

1. ....

2. ....

3. ....

4. ....

5. ....

6. ....

7. ....

8. ....

9. ....

10. ....

C Compare your questions with those in the Answer Key on page 141.

D ▭ Read the text. You should find some of the answers to your questions. When you have finished, listen to the recording to find out more information.

Kangaroos, of which there are over 40 species, are found in Australia, Tasmania and New Guinea. The largest and most common are the grey kangaroo and the red kangaroo, which are often up to 2 metres tall, and can weigh 90 kilograms. They can reach speeds of 60 kilometres per hour, the female being able to hop faster than the male. On average, they jump about 1.5–3 metres at a time, but they can jump 6 metres or more under pressure. They can also jump over fences 3 metres high. They live in grassland and open forests and are herbivores. The young kangaroo or 'joey' lives in its mother's pouch for about six months, and slowly becomes independent of her. The average lifespan of the kangaroo is 15 years; if they live to the maximum age, around 20, or even 30, they probably die of starvation, because their teeth eventually fall out or wear out.

Here are some jokes. Match the questions with the correct answers.

a. What do you know about achondroplasia?
b. What were Tarzan's last words?
c. What do you give a sea-sick hippopotamus?
d. What never asks questions but always gets answered?
e. What is an adult?

1. Someone who has stopped growing at both ends and is expanding in the middle.
2. The phone.
3. It's hard to spell.
4. Who greased that vine?
5. Plenty of space.

Write a paragraph about yourself in the space below, similar to the biography of Paul on page 16 of the Class Book. Include the following information:

– where you were born
– where you grew up
– something about your education
– what you did after you left school
– whether you are married and have children

Try to use *so*, *because* and *because of* in your autobiography.

....
....
....
....
....
....
....
....

9 Speaking partners

A Compare your answers to Exercise 2, Part B.

B Find a form to fill in, either in your own language or in English.

Examples: *driving licence application form*
passport application form
enrolment form for an English language school

With your speaking partner, decide which questions you would need to ask in English in order to complete the form for someone else.

Examples: NAME: *What's your name?*
ADDRESS: *Where do you live?*
DATE OF BIRTH: *When were you born?*

10 Reflections

This space is for you to make a note of things you have learnt in this unit. You can also use it as a diary to write about your problems and progress in English.

....
....
....
....
....
....
....
....
....
....
....
....
....
....

3

STREETLIFE

1 Take the first road on the left

directions

Complete the table below with suitable words and phrases.

Take the	first	road	on the	left.
	....	....		....
	....	....		
Go straight	.................,	until you	get to	the ....
	.................,		....	the ....
Keep going,				the ....
It's on the	left-hand	side of the	....	
	....		....	
It's	opposite	the bank.		
	....			
	....			
	....			
Turn	....	at the	....	
	....		....	
		into	....	
It's just	after	the		
	....	the		
	....	the		

2 It might be Chinese

possibility and probability

Make sentences about these languages, using the expressions of possibility and probability on page 19 of your Class Book.

Example: *Number 1* **is probably** *Asian; it* **might be** *Japanese. Number 2* **is definitely** *Portuguese. (I know a bit of Portuguese.)*

Then check which languages they are in the Answer Key on page 142.

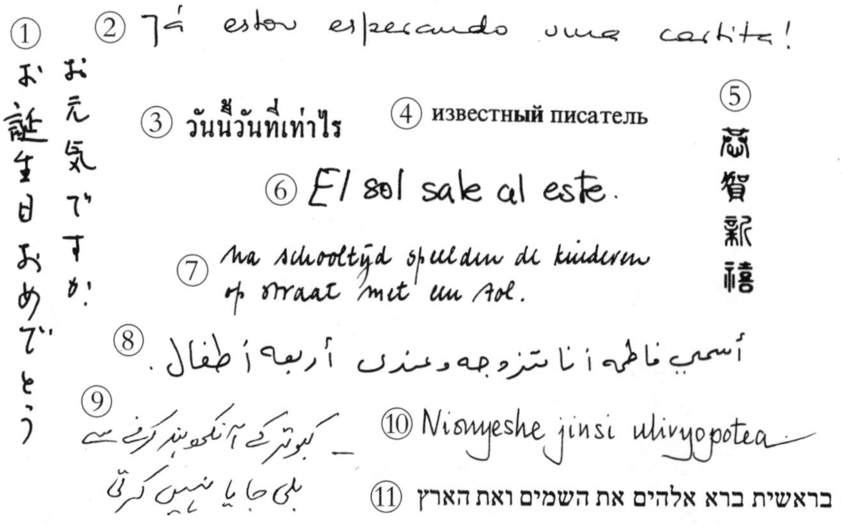

① お誕生日おめでとう お元気ですか!
② Já estou esperando uma cartita!
③ วันนี้วันที่เท่าไร
④ известный писатель
⑤ 恭賀新禧
⑥ El sol sale al este.
⑦ Na schooltijd speelden de kinderen op straat met een bal.
⑧ أسمي فاطمة وأنا متزوجة وعندي أربعة أطفال.
⑨ کبوتر کے آنکھ بند کرنے سے بلی جا یا نہیں کرتی
⑩ Nionyeshe jinsi ulivyopotea
⑪ בראשית ברא אלהים את השמים ואת הארץ

3 Picture dictation

 In this exercise you are going to complete the map below. You need a pencil and a rubber. Now follow the instructions on the recording.

MAIN ROAD

River

4 Dialogues
asking for and giving directions

Complete the dialogues using the map from Exercise 3.
All the conversations begin at the railway station.

1. A: Excuse me, can you tell me where .... is?

   B: Yes, go out of the station, down to the main road, turn left, go over the bridge and

   it's on your left.

   A: ....

2. A: Is .... far from here?

   B: No – turn right, and it's at the end of the road.

3. A: Excuse me, do you know where the Walls Factory is?

   B: ....

   ....

   A: Great. Thanks very much.

4. A: ....?

   B: Yes, go down to the main road, turn left, go straight over the bridge, keep going and

   take the first turning on your right. It's on your left, just in front of you.

   A: ....

5. A: Excuse me, do you know where the mosque is?

   B: ....

   A: OK, never mind. Thanks anyway.

A Check that you understand the words in the box below before you read about the maps.

a stick	coastline	wooden	to represent	a seashell	to carve
a current	a canoe	to land	frontier		

B Match the descriptions below with the pictures. Try not to look in a dictionary.

B

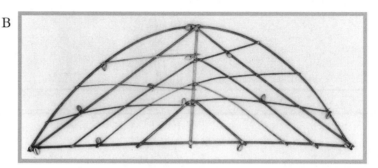

A

C

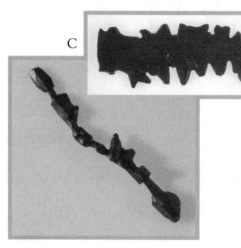

D

1. In the past, maps weren't necessarily drawn on paper. This picture shows a map from the Marshall Islands in the Pacific Ocean. The map is made of thin sticks with seashells attached where the sticks meet or at points along the sticks.

   The shells represent islands or groups of islands in the ocean, and the sticks represent ocean currents, or the course of a canoe. These were, and still are, used for instruction: sailors learnt the 'picture' on land, and could remember it at sea.

2. Early on in the development of map making, you can find the traditional wooden maps of the Eskimos of Greenland. These are pieces of wood with coastlines carved in them. A complete map can be made up of two sticks, one showing the coastline, the other (the larger piece in the illustration) representing the islands off the coast.

   Sometimes the maps also showed where it was easy to land. In any case, these maps could not be used without an explanation from the people who made them.

3. A long time ago, people in China made maps from three-dimensional models. Some were made of wood, and some were used as incense burners and other containers. The map in the picture is in fact an incense burner of the Han dynasty (206 BC–AD 220), and its cover is a mountain. Shen Kua wrote a description of making a three-dimensional map in 1086:

   When I went to see the frontier, I made for the first time a wooden map on which I represented the mountains, rivers and roads. I personally explored the mountains and rivers in the region … I had the map carved in wood and then presented it to the emperor. He then invited all the officials to come and see it, and later ordered similar maps to be made of frontier regions.

4. Some maps, however, are sculptures in 'bas-relief' and are beautiful works of art. The one here, from Nineveh in the 6th century BC, shows a triumphal procession after the capture of a town by Assurbanipal. Around the plan of the town you can see soldiers, musicians and the wheels of a chariot (left). In the centre is a very clear picture map of the town, its walls with houses inside and out, the palm trees around it, houses in the suburbs and the main river with fish visible in the water.

6 A bad sense of direction

Listen to Gareth, Lynn and Ian describing their experiences of getting lost and answer these questions.

	Gareth	Lynn	Ian
Who were they with?	....	....	....
Where did they get lost?	....	....	....
Why did they get lost?	....	....	....
How long were they lost?	....	....	....

7 Postcards

Complete the postcard with words from the box.

take	turn	get	go	get off

Dear Jack,

It'll be great to see you next week, and it's very easy to get to the house.

.... the 57 bus from the station and .... at the market. Then .... along Kendall Street until you .... to the post office. .... left and my road is the second on the right. See you at eight o'clock.

Love,

Binky

Jack Stone

125 Stanneylands Avenue

Wilmslow

Cheshire SK9 4EJ

Write a similar postcard, giving directions to your house, for someone who is coming to visit you. You might need to use a bilingual dictionary to help you. Show it to your teacher if you like.

8 Speaking partners

A Telephone your partner and give them directions to your house in English.

B Do these two exercises when you are travelling to work or school. When you meet your speaking partner, give them the directions and the names of the places you see on the way.

1. On your journey to work or school, practise the directions in your head.

   Example: *Go down to the main road, turn left, go along Koenigstrasse, take the first turning after the castle, …*

2. Try to name in English any buildings or places you see on the way (church, post office, car park, etc.).
   If you don't know the name in English, make a note of it and look it up later, or ask your English teacher or speaking partner.

9 Visual dictionary

Label the pictures on page 120 with the correct preposition. (In several cases there may be more than one possible answer.)

10 Reflections

This space is for you to make a note of things you have learnt in this unit. You can also use it as a diary to write about your problems and progress in English.

....

....

....

....

....

....

....

....

....

....

....

....

....

....

CREATIVITY

1 Missing letters

Complete these sentences by writing the first letter of each word.

Example: _hey _ave _anced _n _ront _f _he _resident.
　　　　 They *have* **d**anced *in* **f**ront **of** **t**he **P**resident.

1. _e _asn't _een _broad _n _is _ife.

2. _he _asn't _t _ome _esterday.

3. _as _nyone _ver _sed a _rick _s a _aperweight?

4. _he _idn't _o _ut _ast _ight.

5. _'ve _ever _ade a _peech _n _ublic.

6. _ere _ou _usy _ast _eek?

7. _ave _ou _ver _layed _ootball _ith _n _range?

8. _e _aven't _een _ny _ood _ilms _ere.

9. _ho _rote _he _ords _or _hat _ong?

10. _e _as _ade _ome _eautiful _rnaments.

2 Dictation

▭ Listen to the four conversations and write them down. Stop the recording where necessary.

When you have finished, look at the verbs in the conversation. Have you written the correct tense? Remember that if we know *when*, we use the past simple and not the present perfect. Check your dictation with the tapescript on page 133.

3 Expressing personal feelings

A Complete the following sentences about yourself.

1. I always apologise when ....

2. I sometimes refuse invitations when ....

3. I get angry when ....

4. Sometimes I feel embarrassed when ....

5. I always try to make a few suggestions when ....

6. And I am always pleased when ....

B Here are six possible endings to the sentences above. Match the two halves and then compare the complete sentences with your own.

a. I'm tired.
b. people take my advice.
c. I meet new people for the first time.
d. people are late for appointments.
e. I'm late for a meeting.
f. people ask me for help or advice.

4 Creative word search

Here are some words you can form out of the word *creative*. Look up any words that are new to you in your dictionary.

ace	act	active	at	car	care	cat	create	eat	erect
ever	ice	race	rat	rate	react	tea	tear	tree	vet

Now see how many words you can form out of the following:

1. breakfast   2. calendar

5 Weak vowels and word stress

A Read the words in the list below aloud. (The stressed syllables are underlined.)

<u>sa</u>lad   a<u>long</u>   <u>car</u>rot   co<u>llapse</u>   <u>bott</u>om   <u>A</u>frica

B Look at the words again. How do you pronounce the unstressed vowels *a* and *o* which are printed in bold?

In fact, the letters *o* and *a* are often pronounced the same way – /ə/ – if they are not part of a stressed syllable.

C Mark the main stress on these words. Which vowels are pronounced /ə/?

angry	confused	embarrassed	umbrella	Japan	connect
apologise	collar	panic	comma		

⬛ Listen to the recording to check your answers and practise saying the words in sentences with the recording.

6 Wake up your brain's creative side!

Read the text and think about the questions at the end of each paragraph while you are reading.

The diagram on the right shows you that the brain has two sides: the left side which controls logical, rational thinking; and the right side which is more dominant in artistic activities which require imagination.

IMAGINATION   RATIONAL THINKING

ARTISTIC ABILITY   LOGIC

Did you know this?

Psychologists believe that most of us have a lot of creative ability, but often we don't use it because our daily lives are dominated by the organised, analytical left side of the brain. And this is particularly true at school where much more time and emphasis is given to left brain activities such as mathematics and verbal reasoning, than to right brain activities such as art and music.

Was your school like this?

What's more, even when we do activities which are more successful using the right side of the brain, we often use the left side instead. An example of this is drawing. Many people try to identify the thing they are drawing, e.g. an eye or a nose, and then copy their idea of what an eye or a nose looks like. In other words, they draw what they know and not what they see. This is an example of left brain thinking and the result is usually very childlike.

Does this happen to you when *you* draw things?

However, you can switch off the left side of the brain when you are drawing by using the following technique, invented by Betty Edwards, who has written a book about learning to draw with the right side of the brain.

Would you like to try this? If so, read on.

1. Find a quiet place to draw; play music if you like. Finish the drawing in one session; give yourself 30–40 minutes, or more if possible.
   Do not turn your drawing the right way up until you've finished.

2. Look at the upside down drawing for a minute. Study the angles and lines; where one line begins, another ends.

line _____ angle

3. When you start drawing, begin at the top. Copy each line. Don't try to name the parts of the drawing; it's not necessary. If you come to parts that you could name, the hands or face, say, just continue to think, 'Well, this line goes that way, this line is like an angle,' and so on.

4. Move from line to line. When you start, you will become very interested in how lines go together. In time, your left brain will switch off and the right brain switch on.

5. After you finish, turn your drawing the right way up. You will probably be surprised at how well the drawing came out.

📖 Find yourself somewhere comfortable to sit, where you can be alone and relax completely. Breathe deeply and regularly, and empty your mind of everything.

When you are ready to take a trip in your mind, play the recording and let your imagination go free.

8 Creative uses

Here are some more creative tests like those in Unit 4 of the Class Book.

A Write down as many uses as possible for the following, using a dictionary if necessary:

 a blanket a bowl

Examples: *You can use a blanket as a shopping bag.*
You can use a blanket to keep you warm.
You can use a bowl as a hat.
You can use a bowl to keep things in.

B In no more than 50 words, complete the short story in one of these three different ways:

a. with a funny ending
b. with a happy ending
c. with a shocking ending.

The town hall was filled with local people, all waiting for their leader to make a speech. Portraits of the great man were all around the room. The evening began with a child reading aloud a poem in honour of the leader. A group of schoolchildren acted out a short play, illustrating the leader's victories and bravery. The moment arrived. The great man got up to speak …

Compare your ending with those on page 143.

9 Speaking partners

A Discuss your answers to the last exercise with your speaking partner.

B Think about your daily lives: your work, your home life, your hobbies. Make a list together of all the creative things you do every day. Some of them may be very small, but still include them.

Examples: *You may be creative in the combination of clothes that you wear every day.*
Perhaps you repair something in a creative way.
Perhaps you find an original solution to a problem at work.

10 Reflections

This space is for you to make a note of things you have learnt in this unit. You can also use it as a diary to write about your problems and progress in English.

....
....
....
....
....
....
....
....
....
....

YOU AND YOUR BODY

1 Break, broke, broken

irregular verbs

Complete the table and check your answers on page 143.

Infinitive	Past tense	Past participle	Infinitive	Past tense	Past participle
break	....	....	take	....	....
feel	....	....	teach	....	....
hurt	....	....	spend	....	....
shake	....	....	bring	....	....
cut	....	....	find	....	....
bend	....	....	know	....	....
throw	....	....	lie (on a bed)	....	....
give	....	....			

Now cover the past tense and past participle columns and test yourself.

2 Enjoy yourself

reflexive pronouns

Complete the sentences with the correct reflexive pronoun.

1. I think she cut .... using that knife.

2. We introduced .... to the guests.

3. I taught .... how to swim.

4. The children can look after ....

5. Did you hurt .... when you fell over?

6. She told us to help .... to the sandwiches.

7. He looked at .... in the bathroom mirror.

8. I must learn to control ....

3 How often do you ...?

frequency adverbs; time expressions

A Number the words and phrases in each box in order of frequency.
Write number 1 next to the most frequent.

A

...... quite often
...... hardly ever
...... never
...... occasionally
...... sometimes

B

...... three times a year
...... once a week
...... every other day
...... every day
...... every couple of months
...... twice a day

B Now answer these questions using the words and phrases above.

How often do you ...
- see a film in English?
- listen to the news in English?
- learn new words?
- do homework?
- write a letter in English?
- revise irregular verbs?

- ask your teacher a question in class?
- speak to your partner in class in English?
- listen to the words of an English song?
- read a magazine or newspaper in English?
- write things down in Reflections at the end of each unit?

Do you want to do any of these more often?

4 I shut my head

vocabulary: collocation

All the underlined verbs are in the wrong sentences. Put each one in the correct place.

1. I <u>shut</u> my head.
2. I <u>pointed</u> my hair.
3. I <u>folded</u> my vitamin pills.
4. I <u>took</u> my finger at him.
5. I <u>had</u> my arms.
6. I <u>combed</u> yoga.
7. I <u>shook</u> my eyes.
8. I <u>felt</u> upstairs.
9. I <u>did</u> a cold.
10. I <u>ran</u> ill.

5 Bathtub pleasure

reading

Read the text below. Write short answers to the questions as you read the text.

Relaxing in a warm bath is one of the best things in life. The Roman Emperor, Gordian had four or five baths a day.

Does that surprise you?

Napoleon Bonaparte used to take very hot baths in the middle of the night, which horrified his doctor. But many people are bath-lovers, lying in the bath long after the washing is finished. When they get out of the bath, they feel relaxed and very much better.

How about you?

One reason why is that your body 'floats' in water, so your muscles can relax. A hot bath can lower the blood pressure too. But *very* hot water isn't so relaxing; in fact, it makes your heart beat faster, and it can take thirty minutes for the body to get back to normal.

Have you ever experienced this?

Craig Sharp, of the British Olympic Medical Centre, says that baths and showers are good for tired muscles, and they make athletes recover from fatigue more quickly.

Does that make sense to you?

Sharp did an experiment to see how athletes feel in different circumstances. He did three different tests:

    a. Some athletes went for a run, then had a cool shower.

    b. Some athletes went for a run, but had no shower afterwards.

    c. Some athletes had no run, but had a shower.

Which do you think created the best feeling among the athletes?

The best feeling was clearly created by the run followed by a cool shower. But to everyone's surprise, a shower alone was superior to a run without a shower. The feeling of cool water on the skin is enough, it seems, to create a gentle feeling of euphoria.

Which would you prefer?

But, it seems, the ritual of bathing is important in our territorial instincts. People like to bathe when they move into a new house, or even a hotel room. Or is it just that we are tired, and need the bath to relax us?

So – when do *you* take a bath or shower?

---

6 When I was in Spain ...

In the Class Book you listened to 'body stories' and told your own.
Stories often have a sequence like this:

This is about an accident that happened when I was in Spain.

Where and when it happened:	....
Information about the situation:	....
Sequence of events in the story:	....
	....
Result of the events:	....

Put these events in the correct order, and then write the complete story in the box.

1   This is about an accident that happened when I was in Spain.
where they cleaned and bandaged my finger.
Just at that moment, I saw a friend across the street.
It was badly cut and terribly painful.
One day I parked my car outside a shop and got out.
My friend rushed over and drove me to the hospital,
Incredibly, I still have the scar today, fifteen years later.
As I said 'hello', I shut my finger in the door.

Now write your own body story, following the sequence in the box.

7 Body factfile

⬚⬚ Listen to the questions on the recording and speak or write your answers. Listen to all the questions, then you can use the tapescript on page 133 to identify any problems of comprehension.

8 Visual dictionary

Draw and label the missing parts in the pictures on page 121.

9 Speaking partners

Compare your answers to Exercise 7 (Body factfile) and your answers to Exercise 3 (How often do you ...?). You can also do one of these activities:

A If you come from the same country, look in your bathroom at any products you use which have information on them in your language and English. For instance, toothpaste, medicines, mouthwash, dental floss, make-up, after-shave, shampoo. Compare the English translation with your own language.

B If you come from different countries, tell each other about the health service in your country. Who pays for health care?

10 Reflections

This space is for you to make a note of things you have learnt in this unit. You can also use it as a diary to write about your problems and progress in English.

....
....
....
....
....
....
....
....
....
....
....
....
....
....

LEARNING – PAST AND PRESENT

1 *I've seen or I saw?*

Complete the sentences using the correct tense.

1. I .... (see) that man every day this week.

2. I .... (save) a bit of money last month, but I'm afraid I ....
   (spend) it all this week.

3. Our teacher .... (give) us a lot of homework last night.

4. They .... (be) to New York twice this year.

5. She .... (speak) to him yesterday.

6. Joan .... (get) back from her holiday last week, but I .... (not
   see) her yet.

7. Three families in our street .... (have) babies so far this year.

8. I .... (come) to Oxford three weeks ago, but so far I .... (not
   eat) any English food at all – just Chinese, Indian or Italian.

9. So far this term we .... (do) six units of our English book.

10. I .... (buy) the car two years ago. At first it .... (be) fantastic, but
    this year I .... (have) lots of problems with it.

11. We .... (not travel) much so far this year, but we .... (have) a
    wonderful time in Portugal last summer.

12. I .... (receive) ten letters this month.

2 Words with more than one meaning

When you look up a word in a dictionary you may find it has several meanings:

Fine can be a verb, a noun or an adjective.
It can also have different meanings. It can be:
– the money you pay when you break the law;
– bright and sunny;
– healthy and comfortable.

**From the pictures, identify two different
meanings for each of the words in the box.
Use a dictionary to check your answers.**

| nail | box | star | glasses |

3 It's such an easy exercise

A Complete the sentences using *so* or *such*.

1. We've got .... a large family that we always have to travel in two cars.

2. He stayed .... a long time that I had to ask him to leave.

3. It was .... wet that we decided to come home.

4. They were .... interesting students that I really enjoyed teaching them.

5. It was .... hot in the theatre that I left before the end of the play.

6. It's .... a nice day that I think I'll go for a walk.

7. The food was .... bad that we couldn't eat it.

8. The sea was .... dangerous that they had to stop people surfing.

B Complete the following sentences using *so* + adjective
or *such (a/an)* + adjective + noun.

Example: ...*The room was so cold*...... that I had to put my coat on.
          or ...*It was such a cold room*.... that I had to put my coat on.

1. .... that we couldn't see a thing.

2. .... that she gave me a big kiss.

3. .... that I couldn't watch.

4. .... that I asked for my money back.

5. .... that I didn't know what to say.

6. .... that I couldn't concentrate at all.

7. .... that I kept making mistakes.

8. .... that I was sorry one team had to lose.

---

4 How to pronounce the letter *u*

Put these words into the correct columns below.

| subject | useless | computer | lunch | just | rule | sunny | adult |
| student | such | unpleasant | use | study | refuse | discuss | confused |

/ʌ/	/uː/	/juː/
e.g. sun	true	tube
....	....	....
....	....	....
....	....	....
....	....	....
....	....	....
....	....	....
....	....	....
....	....	....
....	....	....

You will need three balls of the same size, as shown in the picture. If you haven't got three balls, use three oranges.

Now read and follow the instructions, using the pictures to help you.

Step 1: One ball

An important rule in juggling is that if you get the *throw* right, the *catch* will be easy.
Practise throwing one ball in an easy arc from one hand to the other.
You should throw the ball from about *waist* height to a point level with the top of the head.

(When you throw with *two* balls, they will follow a different trajectory, so they shouldn't hit each other in the air.)

Step 2: Two balls

Hold one ball in each hand. Throw the right hand ball in an arc towards your left hand.
As it gets to the top of the arc, throw the second ball in an arc below it to your left hand.
Catch the balls.
Make sure you throw each ball to the *same* height.

Step 3: Three balls

Hold two balls in your right hand and one in your left.
Throw the *first* ball (1) in your right hand towards the left hand.
As it gets to the top of the arc, throw the ball in your left hand (2) towards the right. Catch the first ball in your left hand.
As the second ball (2) gets to the top of the arc, throw the last ball (3) from your right hand, and then catch the second ball in your right hand.
Repeat this sequence and you are juggling!
Don't be surprised if you don't juggle at your first attempt. Practice makes perfect.

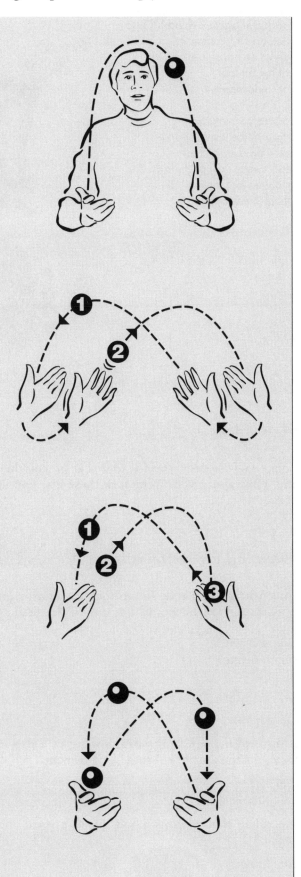

6 Who'd be a juggler?

Read this poem. Use a dictionary to help you.

Last night, in front of thousands of people,
he placed a pencil on his nose
and balanced a chair upright on it
while he spun a dozen plates behind his back.
Then he slowly stood on his head to read a book
at the same time as he transferred the lot
to the big toe of his left foot.
They said it was impossible.

This morning, in our own kitchen,
I ask him to help with the washing-up –
so he gets up, knocks over a chair,
trips over the cat, swears, drops the tray
and smashes the whole blooming lot!
You wouldn't think it was possible.

Cicely Herbert

7 What can you do?

Someone once said about a world leader that he couldn't walk and chew gum at the same time. How about you? Which of these can you do? Listen and say *yes* or *no* or *sometimes*.

8 *Writing, writting, or writeing?*

In the Class Book you learnt a rule about doubling consonants in one-syllable verbs. The same rule works for longer words, but only if the final syllable is stressed.

Examples: begin *beginning*
permit *permitted*
but
visit *visiting*
open *opened*

The exception (in British English) is words ending in *l*: they always double the consonant if they end consonant + vowel + consonant.

Examples: cancel *cancelled*
travel *travelling*

Another spelling rule is that when you add *-ing* to a word ending in *e* (but not *ee*), the final *e* is omitted:

Examples make *making*
hope *hoping*

Correct the spelling mistakes in these sentences.

1. I'm writing to tell you about my traveling arrangements.
2. They offerred him a lot of money for the car.
3. We are planing to go swiming next week. Are you comeing?
4. They canceled the show because a lot of people were ill.
5. The man robed the bank, but then dropped the money when he climbed over a wall. Later he was stoped by the police.
6. I'm hoping to go next week, but I'm not takeing the car because the roads are always so busy.
7. She has forgoten her key again.
8. Why are you useing my dictionary?
9. He admited it was his mistake.
10. When I phoned her she promissed to help.

9 Speaking partners

A Go to your local adult evening institute or night school, where people study different subjects for work or pleasure. Get a list of these subjects and translate them into English (or your own language if you are living in an English-speaking country). Which would you like to learn and why?

B Do Exercise 7 (What can you do?) together. Then try to think of more questions to ask each other like these:

Examples: *Can you cook dinner and watch TV at the same time?*
Can you do your homework and drive at the same time?

10 Reflections

This space is for you to make a note of things you have learnt in this unit. You can also use it as a diary to write about your problems and progress in English.

....
....
....
....
....
....
....
....
....
....
....
....
....
....
....

LETTERS THAT TELL A STORY

1 Lexical pairs

vocabulary

Find pairs of words in the box that are connected in some way:

Examples: *a leopard and a camel*
             (They are both animals.)
             a three star hotel and a guest house
             (They are both types of accommodation.)

leopard	three-star hotel	street	tent	hepatitis	adult	lemons
knife	lake	word processor	fortnight	dustman	week	caravan
pond	sore throat	gun	motorway	camel	guest house	oranges
dentist	teenager	typewriter				

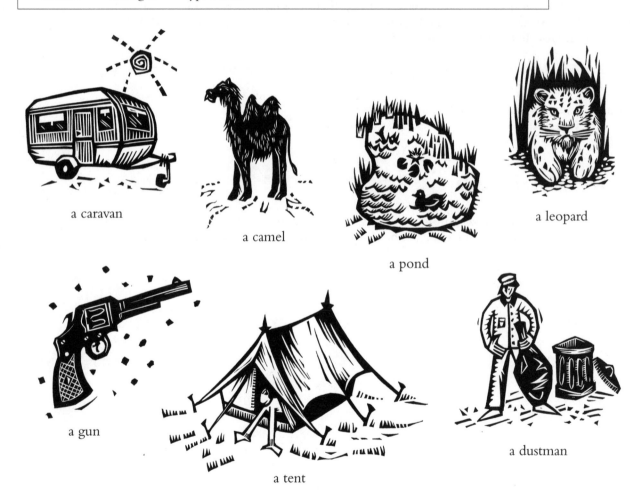

a caravan

a camel

a pond

a leopard

a gun

a tent

a dustman

2 A leopard is faster than a camel

comparatives

Make twelve different comparative sentences using each pair of words from Exercise 1.

Examples: *A leopard is faster than a camel.*
             Hepatitis is more serious than a sore throat.

◫ Now listen to the examples on the recording. Write down any that are different from your own and compare them.

A Use the prefixes to form opposites of the words in the box. Use a dictionary if necessary.

un–   in–   il–   dis–

comfortable	sensitive	formal	honest	popular	organised	
imaginative	expected	legible	friendly	reliable	satisfactory	legal

Example: *uncomfortable*

B Complete these sentences with some of the words you have formed.

1. If nobody likes you, you are ....

2. If you often tell lies, you are ....

3. If you don't consider other people's feelings, you are ....

4. If other people cannot depend on you, you are ....

5. If other people cannot read your handwriting, it is ....

6. If your work isn't good enough, it is ....

7. If something is against the law, it is ....

8. If something happens which is a surprise, it is ....

9. If you often leave things in a mess, you are ....

10. If a word is only used in conversation or to friends, it is ....

Match the words and phrases in the box with the correct text type below. (Some may go with more than one type of text.)

recipe	diary entry	postcard	application form	addressed envelope	formal letter

ring vet	....
lovely weather	....
Yours faithfully	....
Private and Confidential	....
plumber 10.30 am	....
add flour	....
see you soon	....
dental appointment	....
marital status	....
urgent	....
We apologise for the delay	....
one small onion, chopped	....
occupation	....
airmail	....

Graphologists (people who analyse handwriting) divide handwriting into three zones: the middle zone which is the body of small letters, and the upper and lower zones, formed by the extensions of letters such as *f, k, g, y,* and capital letters.

Handwriting

upper zone
middle zone
lower zone

Now match these samples of handwriting with the explanations in the text. Use a dictionary to help you.

a Outside of the prune-industry press, Ive seen very

b 13, newly married also to a very pretty, pleasant young lady.—All

c Now is the time for all good men to

d Doug its took so long to pay some on my bill we will try

e Though no replies, my mind tells me

f of the "to be returned" items

g visiting my friend on Cambridge Pound) and with another friend on

h I am enjoying this party very much.

What do your letters say?

1. Upper zone formations like stick figures suggest that the writer is very practical and realistic. A person who likes facts.

2. A thrust is a sudden movement of the pen from one zone into another. Upward thrusts indicate a person who is constantly thinking and is probably very creative.

3. When the handwriting runs into the lines above and below, the writer may be a bit of a dreamer and perhaps unreliable. But the writer will also have lots of charm and will be popular.

4. If the middle zone is very developed the writer is probably self-confident. Connected writing also suggests someone who is very logical.

5. Small writing with all the zones of the same size shows a writer of independence who can concentrate for very long periods. These writers can be very clever.

6. If the lower zone is very strong the writer may be quite materialistic – interested in money and possessions.

7. A vertical slant suggests the writer is very careful, but often someone with a lot of personal magnetism.

8. The backward slant suggests self-interest. The writer is independent and difficult to understand, but may also have a very charming public personality.

vertical slant

vertical slant

backwards slant

backward slant

🎧 Listen to Lynn and Gareth and complete the table.

	Lynn	Gareth
1. How old were they when they started to learn to write?	....	....
2. What can they remember about it?	....	....
3. Can they write in more than one script?	....	....
4. What do other people think of their writing?	....	....
5. What do they think of it?	....	....

A Do you remember the spelling rule you learnt in the last unit about verbs + *-ing* or + *-ed*? (See Class Book, page 37.) The same rule works for comparative and superlative adjectives, so write down the correct forms for these adjectives.

1. big	bigger	the biggest	5. neat	....	....
2. soft	softer	the softest	6. thin	....	....
3. fat	....	....	7. wet	....	....
4. small	....	....	8. cheap	....	....

B Here is another spelling rule. Adjectives which end consonant + *y*, change the *y* to an *i* before *-er* and *-est*:

Examples: dry   *drier*   *the driest*
            friendly   *friendlier*   *the friendliest*

Complete the following table.

Adjective	Comparative	Superlative
1. ea_ y	....	....
2. bu_ y	....	....
3. ti_ y	....	....
4. fu_ _ y	....	....
5. liv_ _ y	....	....
6. clou _ y	....	....
7. hap_ y	....	....
8. su_ _ y	....	....
9. hea_ y	....	....
10. fo_ _ y	....	....

8 Speaking partners

A Show your partner a piece of your handwriting from your exercise book. Together, look at the text in Exercise 5, and analyse your handwriting. Then say if you think it is a true interpretation.

B Ask each other the questions in Exercise 6. Can you think of any other questions to ask about this subject?

9 Reflections

This space is for you to make a note of things you have learnt in this unit. You can also use it as a diary to write about your problems and progress in English.

....

....

....

....

....

....

....

....

....

....

....

....

....

....

8

TAKE IT OR LEAVE IT

1 Are you busy this evening?

ways of expressing the future

Put the verbs in brackets into the correct form. You need *will*, *going to* or the present continuous. More than one answer is possible in some cases.

1.

A: Are you busy this evening?

B: Yes, I .... (meet) a couple of friends from work. Would you like to join us?

A: Well, I .... (watch) the football on TV until about nine, but maybe I could meet you later.

B: Why don't you video the football, then you could spend the whole evening with us?

A: Yes, that's a good idea. Right I .... (do) that.

2.

A: Has Bob decided about next year?

B: Yes, he .... (do) voluntary work in Africa.

A: Mm, sounds interesting. How about Belinda?

B: Oh, she .... (stay) at college for another year. After that, I don't think she knows what she .... (do). But why don't you ask her yourself, she's upstairs.

A: Well, I'm in a bit of a hurry – I .... (meet) some clients in the city. But I .... (have) a quick word with her.

B: OK, great. You stay there and I .... (call) her.

3.

A: Did you know that Bill and Pam .... (open) a restaurant in the high street?

B: No, I had no idea. But I .... (have) lunch with them next week, so they can tell me all about it.

A: Great. You can tell me, then.

B: Sure, I .... (give) you a ring on Wednesday evening. OK?

2 Could you ring me back?

Back with the meaning *return* is used with a number of verbs in English. Complete the sentences below with the verbs from the box.

take	have	be	send	ring	pay	bring	put	come	go

1. There was something wrong with the jumper so I .... it back to the shop.
2. If I lend you the money, can you .... me back next week?
3. I'm going now but I should .... back by seven o'clock.
4. You can take the books home this evening, but .... them back tomorrow.
5. I phoned him this morning and he promised to .... me back.
6. I asked the shop assistant if I could .... my money back.
7. I enjoyed my holiday in Switzerland very much, so I'm planning to .... back next year.
8. They enjoyed their holiday here, but I don't think they'll .... back.
9. I posted the cheque on Monday, but they .... it back because I forgot to sign it.
10. If you borrow a book, please make sure you .... it back on the shelf.

3 Paraphrasing

Can you think of another way to say the underlined phrases? The answers can all be found in Unit 8 in the Class Book.

Example: I don't have enough money to buy that coat.
          I can't afford that coat.

1. I'm afraid these trousers aren't the right size.
2. I'll have to go back to the shop with it.
3. There's a problem with this radio.
4. I got undressed and lay down.
5. Can I have a refund, please?
6. Where can I try these on?
7. Do you have proof of payment?
8. I'm sorry, but I can't come this evening.
9. Could I borrow some money?
10. Do you have to pay for doctors and medical treatment?

4 Sounds similar

⊂⊃ Read the sentences and then listen to the recording. Are the sentences you hear the same or different? Underline any differences.

1. I'm leaving now and don't try and stop me!
2. I can't afford it at the moment.
3. Are you going to try and get your money back?
4. My sister's lending me the money.
5. We'll have to take it back tomorrow.
6. I'll pay for it in cash.
7. I'm seeing her today.
8. I'll work for nothing.

Check your answers and then repeat the sentences after the recording.

Read the texts about shops in London and decide where you could probably buy the following:

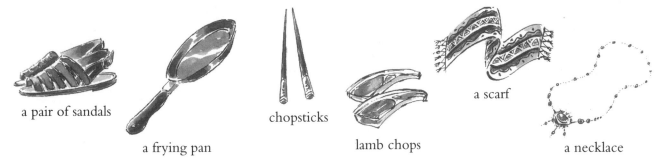

a pair of sandals

a frying pan

chopsticks

lamb chops

a scarf

a necklace

You don't need to know all the vocabulary to answer the questions and have a general understanding of the texts.

Bartholdi The Bartholdi family have had a shop here for over sixty years, and as far as I know are the only Swiss butchers in London. They make and smoke their own sausages, and sell a wide range of delicatessen, specialising in Swiss cheeses as well as selling preserves, continental cakes and tinned groceries.

Kiku There are several Kikus in London, selling decorative and functional items from Japan. These include polyester and cotton kimonos for men, women and children; toys and traditional games; rice bowls, tea sets and mugs.

Divertimenti A specialist kitchen shop which imports practical, well-made utensils and tableware mainly from France. This includes a wide range of cutlery, Sabatier kitchen knives, English and French porcelain, and specialist cooking equipment. Everything is laid out for easy self-service, and there is a colour catalogue which means you can study the goods at home before going to the shop to buy anything.

Turak Turak is located in fashionable St Christopher's Place, just off Oxford Street. It has a wonderful collection of old jewellery. It sells modern gems as well, but the bulk of the stock is antique hand-made jewellery from Afghanistan, Ethiopia, India, Morocco and the Yemen. Many pieces are made of silver, and decorated with coloured stones.

Inca This shop was owned by a Peruvian and later sold to an Englishman. Inca imports a range of Peruvian knitwear and crafts. You can buy brightly-coloured and beige, grey and cream knits (e.g. sweaters, gloves and hats), but they also sell beautiful hand-made wool, baskets, rugs and other decorative objects.

Deliss Deliss make imaginative boots, shoes and handbags in their basement workshop. Their greatest claim is to be able to make a pair of boots in 24 hours. It's best to visit the workshop yourself to see the kind of things they make, which also includes travel bags.

---

6 Listen and answer   listening

🎧 Listen to the recording and answer the questions, either orally or by writing the answers. Listen again if you don't understand a question. At the end, check any questions you don't understand in the tapescript on page 134.

7 Skeleton story

Write out this story, adding words where necessary and using the correct tenses of the verbs.

Example: last week   shopping   city centre
Last week I went shopping in the city centre.

see   trousers   decide   try on   take back   shop   ask   refund

....

pay   cash   get   receipt   assistant   want   see   receipt

....

take   home   discover   problem   give   me   money   back   immediately

....

8 Speaking partners

A Before you meet, make a list of all the things you have bought in the last week, and the kind of shop you bought them in. If necessary, use a bilingual dictionary to help you.

Examples: *matches – at a kiosk*
              a pair of tights – in a department store

Tell your speaking partner what you bought, and see if they know the kind of shop in English. Teach them any new words.

B Together, write two shopping lists in English of things you need to buy in the next few days. When you go to the shops, take your list.

9 Visual dictionary

Complete your visual dictionary on page 122.

10 Reflections

This space is for you to make a note of things you have learnt in this unit. You can also use it as a diary to write about your problems and progress in English.

....

....

....

....

....

....

....

....

....

....

FOOD AND DRINK

1 Correct my mistakes
present simple passive

Correct the grammar mistakes in these sentences.

1. Japanese *sake* usually serves warm.
2. Coffee is often drink after meals.
3. Cola made from cola nut and cocoa.
4. 492 million bottles of Coca-Cola drink every day.
5. In some countries tea is serve with lemon and honey.
6. Coffee is not normally grow in cool climates.
7. How much tea export every year from Sri Lanka?
8. In some countries, stamps are sell in a tobacconist's.

2 Dialogue completion
have to, don't have to, must(n't) and should(n't)

Complete these dialogues, using *have to*, *don't have to*, *must(n't)* or *should(n't)*.

1. A: Would you like to come for a drink?

   B: I'd love to, but I'm afraid I .... go home and get the dinner ready.

   A: Yes, I know, but you .... go home right now, do you?

2. A: I'm not sleeping very well at the moment.

   B: Well, maybe you .... take sleeping pills.

   A: But surely I .... take them without seeing my doctor first?

3. A: Shall I heat up the soup?

   B: No, you .... – we can have it cold, if you like.

4. A: Do you want me to drive?

   B: Yes, OK. But remember that you .... drink if you are going to drive.

5. A: Shall I go out and do the shopping?

   B: No, you .... carry heavy shopping bags with your bad back.

6. A: Can I go to the disco in these jeans?

   B: No, and you .... wear a tie; otherwise, they won't let you in.

3 Verbs with two objects

A In the sentences below, the words *customer*, *waiter*, and *chef* are often in the wrong places. Change them and make the sentences logical.

Example: *The ~~chef~~ showed the customer the menu.* (*waiter* written above *chef*)

chef   waiter   customer

1. The chef ordered the meal.
2. The customer cooked the chef a steak.
3. The waiter brought the chef the first course.
4. The customer served the chef the main course.
5. The chef poured the waiter a glass of wine.
6. The customer offered the waiter a dessert from the trolley.
7. The customer gave the chef the bill.
8. The chef paid the bill and left the customer a tip.

B In the example above, the *customer* is the indirect object and the *menu* is the direct object. If the indirect object comes second, you need a preposition:

Examples: *The waiter showed the menu **to** the customer.*
*The chef cooked a steak **for** the customer.*

Complete these sentences in a suitable way using *to* or *for* after the direct object.

1. He cooked a meal ....
2. I showed the pictures ....
3. She poured some wine ....
4. They gave the money ....
5. I offered the job ....
6. We left a tip ....
7. I sent the tickets ....
8. He served the food ....

4 Food

Look through the words in the box and then answer the questions below. Each time you answer a question, you should put a line through the word or words.

Example: *something you put in the top of a wine bottle.* **cork**

fish	strawberries	lobster	onions	bacon	ham	peppers	cutlery	
avocado	pineapple	menu	starter	garlic	cucumber	beans	lamb	
pork	cabbage	fork	duck	mango	snails	recipe	main course	spoon
peaches	lettuce	bill	~~cork~~	mustard	grapes	dessert	knife	

Can you find:

1. a fruit which is heart-shaped, one that is round and one that can be green or black?
2. all the green foods?
3. things you can't eat the peel of?
4. all the things that were once living creatures?
5. three things you can read?
6. all the things you eat with?
7. three parts of a meal?

One word is left. What is it?

These passages are all from tourist guides to different countries. Read them quickly and guess where they are from.

Are any of the drinks mentioned common in your country?

1 Alcoholic beverages of all kinds are expensive here compared with most western countries. They are sold in local shops without restrictions, and beer is the favourite alcoholic drink. This is usually brewed in German or Czech style. Imported whiskies and wines are available, especially in larger cities. Brandy is particularly expensive. The traditional drink is, of course, *sake* (pronounced 'sah-kay') and is very pleasant with food or on its own. It is served hot in small flasks from which it is poured into little cups. It is actually made from rice which has been cooked in water and fermented, rather like beer, although it has an alcohol content of up to 17%.

2 Wine is the regular drink, whether it is red, white or rosé. Even the cheapest wines are drinkable. In restaurants, the price of wines is surprisingly high for a country where it is so cheap in the shops. In the north, cider is extremely popular. It is the standard accompaniment to a meal of crêpes, and there are a lot of local varieties, most of them very dry and very wonderful. A cider made with pears is also made on a small scale and is not commercially distributed. Most of the beers you will find are in fact Belgian or German.

3 Most drinking in the capital is done in the very cosy 'brown bars' and the beverage most often drunk is beer. This is usually served in small measures (0.25cl) and tends to have a lot of froth. Jenever is a kind of gin, but less strong. It is served in small glasses and is traditionally drunk in one mouthful. Other drinks you see include many liqueurs, especially advocaat (egg flip) and sweet blue curaçao. Beer and jenever are both extremely cheap if bought by the bottle from the supermarket.

4 Coffee is undoubtedly the number one drink and small cups of black coffee ('tinto') are served everywhere. You can also get milky coffee. Tea, however, is not very popular, though herb teas made with mint or camomile are very cheap and good. Beer is very popular and quite good. There are several local brands of which Aguila, Poker, Bavaria and Club Colombia are the most common. There is some imported wine from other countries in South America such as Argentina or Chile. There is a spirit called 'aguardiente' which is very popular, 'Cristal', 'Nectar' and 'Medellin' being the best known.

6 What's on the menu?

📼 Listen to the conversations on the recording, and complete the dialogues.

1. A: What's the soup of the day?

   B: ....

   A: Fine, I'll have that.

2. A: What's Chicken à la Basque, exactly?

   B: ....

   ....

   A: That sounds nice – I'll have that.

3. A: What's in the Salad Provençale?

   B: Well, it's a bit like Salad Niçoise. It's got ....

   ....

   A: Egg?

   B: ....

   A: OK. I'll have that. It sounds interesting.

4. A: What flavour ice cream have you got?

   B: Um, there's ....

   A: Oh, could I ....

   B: Yes, of course.

5. A: What's Pizza della Casa, exactly?

   B: ....

   A: Fine. I'll have that.

   B: Very good, sir.

Did you hear any new words? If so, check how to spell them in the tapescript on page 134, and check what they mean in a dictionary.

7 Sequencing events

Look at this example:

It was a delicious meal. **First** *we had the mushroom soup.* **Then** *I had lobster and Mary had the roast lamb with spring vegetables – she loves lamb.* **After that** *we both had cheese and dessert.* **Finally** *we had coffee and I drank a very large cognac. Mary drove home.*

The words and phrases in bold are often used to sequence a series of events or actions. Turn the following notes into complete sentences and join them with the words and phrases above.

An Evening Out
1. Italian restaurant   quick pizza
2. cinema   the latest film starring Kevin Costner
3. a couple of drinks   bar
4. Joao's flat   listen to music

Now write a description of a pleasant day or evening you had recently. Use the words and phrases above to connect your ideas.

8 Speaking partners

A In your own country you may see menus written in your language *and* English. Each of you should find a menu in your area which is only written in your own language. Then look together at how much of it you can translate into English, using a dictionary. (If you are studying in an English-speaking country, find a menu in English and see how much of it you can translate into your own language.)

B Tell your partner everything you can about these:

1. the best meal you have ever eaten
2. the worst meal you have ever eaten
3. food you like very much, food you hate
4. what you are going to eat for breakfast, lunch or dinner in the next 24 hours
5. your attitude to food: do you live to eat, or do you eat to live? Or is it somewhere in the middle?

9 Visual dictionary

Complete the visual dictionary for this unit on page 123.

10 Reflections

This space is for you to make a note of things you have learnt in this unit. You can also use it as a diary to write about your problems and progress in English.

....

....

....

....

....

....

....

....

....

....

....

....

....

....

FEELINGS: THE GOOD, THE BAD AND THE UGLY

1 Make a suggestion

could

Make two suggestions using *could* about each of the situations in the pictures. Then compare them with the suggestions on page 146.

Example: Picture 1: *He could stop another driver and ask for help.*
He could walk to the nearest phone box and phone a garage.

A In Unit 10 of the Class Book, there are several uses of *get*. Complete the diagrams below, using the words in the box.

depressed a driving licence tired a letter flu annoyed some money from the bank a phone call something to eat a bill hepatitis a washing machine

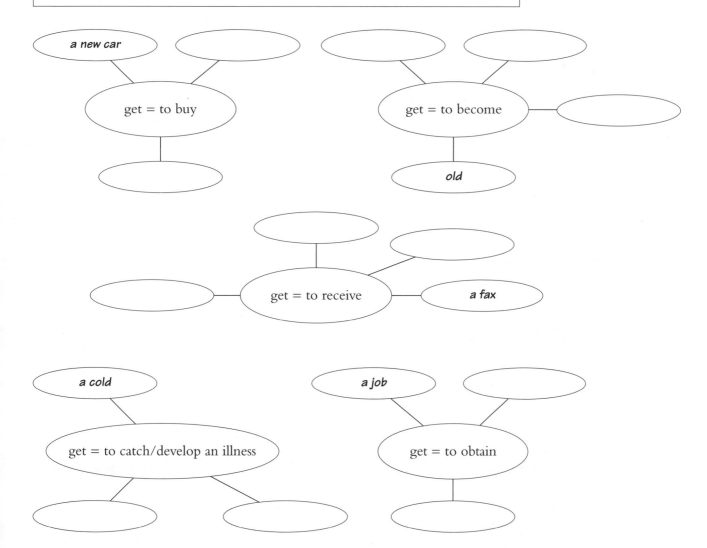

B Complete these sentences with words from the box.

1. I got .... from my sister in Hong Kong last night; it woke me up.

2. I get .... when I speak a lot of English.

3. Look out! You nearly killed that woman on the bike. How on earth did you get your

   ....?

4. Don't worry about cooking for me; I'll get .... on my way home from work.

5. I get very .... when people push in front of me in a queue.

6. I got a very big electricity .... last week.

7. I don't want to get .... again this winter, so I'm going to have a vaccination.

8. Some women get .... after they have a baby.

3 What did they say?

Rewrite the sentences below, but use the verbs in the box and keep the meaning the same.

enjoy	refuse	decide	don't mind	avoid	intend	give up
can't stand	regret					

Example: *He was angry with her so he didn't help.*
He was angry with her so he refused to help.

1. She stopped smoking a year ago.

   ....

2. His plan is to go to California in the summer.

   ....

3. She said it was great to see Bill.

   ....

4. He took a taxi because he was late.

   ....

5. She hates getting up early.

   ....

6. She is sorry she left school at 16.

   ....

7. He is prepared to walk if necessary.

   ....

8. I try not to go to work when the traffic is bad.

   ....

4 Sounds missing

When a word ends with a consonant and the next word begins with the same consonant, we often put the two sounds together, and only say it once.

Examples: *He's the best teacher.*
(We don't pronounce both 't's – /besti:tʃə/.)
She wore a dark coat.
(We don't pronounce the 'k' and the 'c' – /da:kəʊt/.)

⫐ Listen and write down the sentences. Then compare them with the tapescript on page 134, and practise saying them in the same way after the recording.

1. ....

2. ....

3. ....

4. ....

5. ....

6. ....

7. ....

8. ....

Read the quotations about happiness and use a dictionary to help you. Which ones do you agree with?

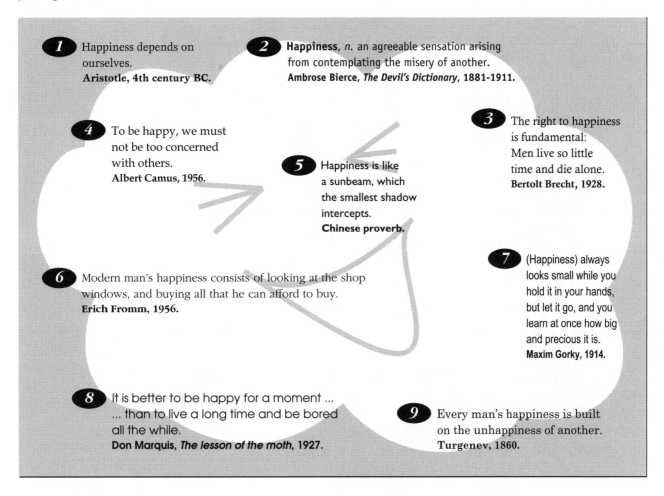

1 Happiness depends on ourselves.
Aristotle, 4th century BC.

2 **Happiness**, *n.* an agreeable sensation arising from contemplating the misery of another.
Ambrose Bierce, *The Devil's Dictionary*, 1881-1911.

3 The right to happiness is fundamental: Men live so little time and die alone.
Bertolt Brecht, 1928.

4 To be happy, we must not be too concerned with others.
Albert Camus, 1956.

5 Happiness is like a sunbeam, which the smallest shadow intercepts.
Chinese proverb.

6 Modern man's happiness consists of looking at the shop windows, and buying all that he can afford to buy.
Erich Fromm, 1956.

7 (Happiness) always looks small while you hold it in your hands, but let it go, and you learn at once how big and precious it is.
Maxim Gorky, 1914.

8 It is better to be happy for a moment ... ... than to live a long time and be bored all the while.
Don Marquis, *The lesson of the moth*, 1927.

9 Every man's happiness is built on the unhappiness of another.
Turgenev, 1860.

📼 Listen to the people on the recording. How do these things make them feel?

	The speakers' feelings
physical exercise	
chocolate	
cool beer	
rock music	
wine	
the colour green	
raw egg	
hot weather	
public transport	
the colour blue	
birthdays	

A Complete the letter using the correct form of a verb from the box.

be	marry	hear	live	give up	make	do	listen
get	watch						

Dear Abby,

I'm writing to ask your advice about my relationship with my girlfriend.
I really want this one to be successful – I have to try to avoid
.... the mistakes I made in the past.

Let me begin by telling you that she's a wonderful person. I enjoy
.... with her and I can't imagine ....
without her. But we have two big problems. First, I'm a musician, and
she can't stand .... to loud music. (I need to play it loud
to really feel it.) Secondly, she is a television critic, and she works at
home, and I hate .... television. I think it's chewing gum
for the mind.

What do you advise? I don't mind .... a few things to
please her, but I refuse .... my job. And it's beginning to
become a real problem, because I'd like .... her but I
don't think she wants .... married just now.

I hope .... from you soon.

Yours sincerely,

Jack Blades

B Continue this reply to Jack. Remember that you use *should* to give advice, and *could* to make suggestions.

Dear Jack,

Thank you for your letter in which you explain your worries about your relationship. It's not unusual for two people to have different interests, and I think ....

....

....

....

....

....

....

....

....

8 Speaking partners

A Look at the list of things in Exercise 6. How do they make *you* feel? Tell your speaking partner. Add three more things to the list, and ask your partner about them.

B Look together at the happiness quotations in Exercise 5. Which do you agree with and why? Can you think of a better definition of happiness?

9 Visual dictionary

Match the verbs in Box A with a word from Box B on page 124 and then label the pictures.

10 Reflections

This space is for you to make a note of things you have learnt in this unit. You can also use it as a diary to write about your problems and progress in English.

....

....

....

....

....

....

....

....

....

....

....

....

....

11

WEATHER

1 What's it like?

vocabulary: word building

Complete the table. Use a dictionary to help you.

Noun	Adjective	Noun	Adjective
climate	....	shower	....
sun	....	ice	....
wind	....	mist	....
cloud	....	....	hot
fog	....	....	cold
....	humid	thunder	....

2 Quantity

too, enough, too much/many

A Complete these sentences using *too, enough, too many* or *too much*.

1. There wasn't .... snow, so we couldn't ski.

2. We were .... busy to have lunch.

3. Have you got .... money for the fare?

4. We decided not to go because there were .... people.

5. It's a pity, but he isn't old .... to be a member.

6. We all ate .... food and had to go to sleep.

7. Sorry I didn't phone you yesterday but I had .... things to do.

8. I couldn't understand the recipe – it was .... complicated, so I made something else.

9. This coffee is very sweet. There's .... sugar in it.

10. We wanted to move into that flat, but there were .... problems with it.

B Using *too, too much, too many* and *enough*, write down reasons why your English may not get better as quickly as you want.

Examples: *I don't have **enough time** to practise.*
*English pronunciation is **too difficult**.*

1. ....

2. ....

3. ....

4. ....

5. ....

3 Hot and cold countries

Which of the things in the list are more important in a hot country, and which are more important in a cold country?

Put the words in the circles.

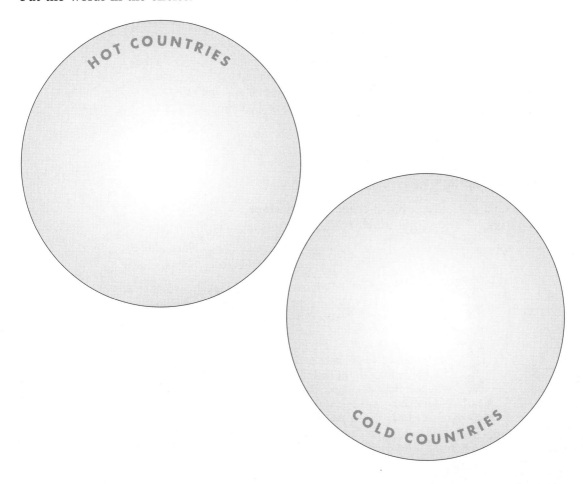

HOT COUNTRIES

COLD COUNTRIES

suntan lotion	fans	T-shirts	blankets	short-sleeved shirts	umbrellas
gloves	soft drinks	woollen scarves	boots	socks	air conditioning
overcoats	central heating	ice cubes			

4 Learning English keeps me busy

Complete these sentences in a suitable way, and then compare them with the possible answers on page 147.

Regular exercise keeps you ....

An electric blanket keeps you ....

A positive attitude to life keeps you ....

An umbrella stops you ....

Too much noise stops you ....

Tranquillisers stop you ....

Drinking wine can ....

Smoking can ....

Sleeping pills can ....

A Every country has popular sayings about the weather. Can you finish the British sayings below? Remember that each one must rhyme.

---

1. Red sky at night,
   Shepherd's delight,
   Red sky ....,
   Shepherd's warning.

2. Rain before seven,
   Clear before ....

3. Long notice, long last,
   Short notice, soon ....

4. If Candlemas Day* is fair and bright,
   Winter will have another fight.
   If Candlemas Day brings cloud and rain,
   Winter is gone and won't come ....

   * = February 2nd.

B Read the text. For each of the four sayings above, is there:

a. a lot of truth in the saying?   c. a bit of truth in the saying?
b. some truth in the saying?   d. not much truth at all in the saying?

PEOPLE have tried to forecast the weather for thousands of years. Our ancestors watched for signs in the sky or special behaviour in animals, and many people still believe these indicators more than weather forecasts on television. Modern research has shown that some of these indicators are useful, but others are nonsense.

Red sky at night,
Shepherd's delight,
Red sky in the morning,
Shepherd's warning.

This means that if the sky is red at sunset, the next day will be fine; but if the sky is red in the morning, it will probably rain. There is some truth in this, because if the sky is red at night, the clouds are probably moving away. On the other hand, if the sky is red in the morning, the clouds have only just arrived.

Rain before seven,
Clear before eleven.

This rule works if weather systems are moving quickly, but there is nothing significant about the time of day. It would be equally true to say 'Rain before one, clear before five', but that doesn't rhyme. All the rule really says is that rain lasts for four hours. This is sometimes true, but often not.

Long notice, long last,
Short notice, soon past.

This is a good general rule. If we know for several days that rain is coming – increasing clouds and a fall in the barometer – then the rain will probably last for several days. If bad weather comes very suddenly, it usually goes very quickly as well.

Many people believe that animals are good at forecasting the weather. It is said that cows lie down before a storm; rabbits sit looking in one direction before a thunderstorm; and cats wash themselves thoroughly when it is going to rain. If these things are true, it is not because animals can predict the weather, but because they are more sensitive to changes of humidity or air pressure.

Most countries have their sayings about the weather, and often they say exactly the same thing. For example, there is a rule for Candlemas Day (2nd February):

If Candlemas Day is fair and bright,
Winter will have another fight.
If Candlemas Day brings cloud
*   and rain,*
Winter is gone and won't come again.

This saying, of course, will not be the same in countries in the southern hemisphere. In actual fact, it is never possible to predict the weather on the basis of a single day, but there is usually just enough truth in many of these sayings for them to remain popular for hundreds of years.

Do certain weather conditions make you feel physically different or ill? If so, you aren't alone. Many people suffer from an illness called 'SAD' which stands for 'Seasonal Affective Disorder'.

Listen to a doctor talking about SAD and complete the sentences.

1. The symptoms of SAD usually include the following:

a. .... d. eating more;

b. the desire to sleep all the time; e. ....

c. ....

2. SAD is thought to be caused by ....

3. SAD usually affects people who live in places with ....

4. A common treatment for SAD is ....

---

7 Advertising slogans

Read these advertisements and look at the pictures.

GAS FIRED HEATING
It keeps you warm when you need it most (cat not included).

COOL CREAM LOTION

When it's hot on the beach, you're cool and calm. Cool cream stops you burning and keeps you young and beautiful.

Now write some advertising slogans for these products.
Try to use *keep somebody/something* + adjective, and *stop something* + *-ing* form.

QUICKSLIM

SOFTSKIN

WINTERWARMER BOOTS

8 Speaking partners

A Try to keep a detailed record of the weather in English over the next seven days. At the end, compare your record with your speaking partner's.

B Get a recent newspaper written in your own language. Find a map or table telling you about the weather around the world. Look at the weather in two or three different English-speaking countries, and translate the information into English.

Does your paper tell you:
— which is the hottest place?
— which is the coldest?
— which is the wettest?
— which is the sunniest?

Work with your speaking partner. If you are of different nationalities, compare what your newspapers say. If you are of the same nationality, translate the information together.

9 Visual dictionary

Complete the visual dictionary for this unit on page 125.

10 Reflections

This space is for you to make a note of things you have learnt in this unit. You can also use it as a diary to write about your problems and progress in English.

....
....
....
....
....
....
....
....
....
....
....
....
....
....

12

ROMANCE

Put the verbs in brackets into the past simple or past continuous.

1. About four weeks ago, I .... (arrive) home at my usual time after

   lunch. My next-door neighbour .... (paint) the wall outside his house

   so I .... (stop) for a quick chat. Then I .... (go)

   inside to read the paper for a few minutes before I .... (start) work.

   One of the cats .... (sit) on a cushion on the radiator while the other

   .... (chase) a fly round the lounge; a normal day.

   I .... (go) into the kitchen to make a cup of tea and – the back door

   .... (be) wide open. Oh, no! I .... (rush) upstairs

   into the front bedroom and then I .... (realise) it

   .... (be) true ....

   ....

2. We .... (walk) along the path

   and .... (put up) our

   tent by the side of the lake. By this time, the sun

   .... (go down) and it

   .... (begin) to get cold.

   While we .... (cook) our

   dinner, we suddenly .... (hear)

   a terrible noise at the far end of the valley.

   We both .... (look up) and

   to our horror we .... (see)

   about 20 cows that .... (run)

   in our direction. 'Let's get out of here!' I

   .... (shout), but when I

   .... (look round),

   ....

   ....

   ....

Now finish both the stories yourself.

Complete the story below with these prepositions:

in	on	at	of	to	by	during	with

An English friend .... mine, Ian, was staying .... friends .... America. One
night, while he was having a drink .... a bar, he met an English woman called Jane. They
spent a lot .... time together .... Ian's holiday and got on very well, but when he left
he didn't write down Jane's address .... England.

  Two months later, ... August, when Ian was relaxing .... holiday .... Corfu,
he met an Irish woman called Elizabeth. They had a great time together and .... the end
.... the holiday they exchanged addresses. .... coincidence, Elizabeth lived very close
.... Ian's parents .... Manchester, so when he went to visit them .... October,
he decided to call on Elizabeth .... the same time. He rang the bell to her flat, but when
the door opened …

Can you remember how the story ends? Look at the full story in your Class Book to
see if you have got all the prepositions correct.

Find a suitable noun from the right for each of the adjectives on the left.

Adjectives   *Nouns*
country   rose
dark   couple
steep   party
middle-aged   forest
romantic   coincidence
amazing   path
red   smile
nervous   lane
surprise   scene
narrow   hill

A Link phrases from the left with phrases from the right using *when* or *while*. (Both are possible in all sentences.)

1. I fell off my bike
2. My legs got burnt
3. I dropped a plate
4. The zip broke
5. I made a mistake
6. The filling came out
7. The windscreen shattered
8. The kettle exploded

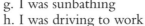

when

while

a. I was getting dressed
b. I was drying the dishes
c. I was adding up the figures
d. I was boiling some water
e. I was cleaning my teeth
f. I was riding to school
g. I was sunbathing
h. I was driving to work

B Now complete each of the sentences using *but fortunately* or *and unfortunately*.

Example: *I fell off my bike while I was riding to school, but fortunately I didn't hurt myself.*
or
I fell off my bike when I was riding to school and unfortunately I broke my ankle.

💿 Listen to the examples on the recording and compare them with your own.

5 How many words?   listening and pronunciation

A 💿 Listen to the recording and write down the number of words in each sentence. When you have finished, look at the tapescript on page 135 and check your answers.

B 💿 Listen again. How are these words pronounced in the sentences?

1. at   2. for   3. of   4. were   5. was   6. of   7. to   8. for

Practise saying the sentences after the recording.

Read the two love letters written by famous English writers, and answer the questions below.

Evelyn Waugh to Laura Herbert, 4 August, 1936
Evelyn Waugh, 1903–66, novelist; Laura Herbert, later his wife.

Grand Hotel Subasio
Assisi
Tuesday

My Darling Laura,
    How I wish you were here. It is a lovely little town – full of sun, you would like that, and bulls and Giottos (he is a famous dead painter). A charming little hotel, a room with a big stone balcony giving onto an empty colonnaded square with directly opposite the church of St Francis. (He is a famous dead saint who put this town on the map.) Good cooking and wine on a terrace from which we can see the whole of Umbria. Mosquitoes all night. Otherwise perfect. If I ever marry I shall bring my wife here for a bit.
    Sweet darling, it seems such a waste to see lovely things and not be with you. It is like being one-eyed and seeing everything out of focus. I miss you and need you all the time. Most of all when I'm happy.

Evelyn

Broadway Central Hotel
New York
Saturday 31st May
6–7 pm

    We got into dock at 8.30 this morning and then there was a lot of waiting about for the luggage: and finally I got here. And it's a beastly hotel: and I'm in a beastly room where there's a hell of a noise: and I've been walking round this damned city all day and riding in its cars (when they weren't too full): and it's hot: and I'm very tired and angry: and my pyjamas haven't come: and I don't know anyone in New York: and I don't like the food: and I don't like the newspapers: and I haven't a friend in the world: and nobody loves me: and I'm going to be extraordinarily miserable these six months: and I want to die.*
    There!
    It's Saturday evening and if I were in England I might be lying on the sofa in Kensington, and my head in your lap, and your face bent down over mine, and your hands about my head, and my eyes shut, and your kind lips wandering over my face. And I'm here in a dirty room and lonely and tired and ill, and this won't get to you for ten days.
    I'm crying. I want you. I don't want to be alone.

Rupert

| *beastly = horrible |

Rupert Brooke to Cathleen Nesbitt, 31 May, 1913
Rupert Brooke, 1887–1915, poet; Cathleen Nesbitt, actress.

Are the following statements true or false?

1. Evelyn Waugh is married.
2. Rupert Brooke arrived by ship.
3. Rupert Brooke is unhappy about the insects.
4. Evelyn Waugh wants to be in England.
5. They both miss the woman they are writing to.
6. Evelyn Waugh is in a hotel with a wonderful view.
7. Rupert Brooke is in a quiet hotel.
8. They both feel it's too hot.

Why I didn't get you a Valentine's card

because I'm into saving trees
because my declarations are not determined by the calendar
because ultimately my heart is my own
because I forgot.

John Hegley

▭ Now complete this poem yourself and compare it with the poem on the recording. You could also exchange poems with your speaking partner.

Why I didn't send you a birthday card

because ....

because ....

because ....

because I forgot.

---

8 Speaking partners

A If you are in your own country, go into a shop that sells greeting cards. Write down as many messages as you can, and then with your speaking partner, translate them into English. Compare with the examples below taken from English cards.

Get well soon   Welcome to your new home   Good luck in your new job
Congratulations!   Many happy returns   Happy Christmas   Best of luck
Happy Anniversary   Sorry I forgot your birthday   Best wishes
Happy Birthday   Happy New Year   With deepest sympathy

B If you are in an English-speaking country, each of you should get a magazine which has a romantic short story in it. (There are many magazines that have stories like this.) Read the story, then tell it to your partner. Is it a good story?

---

9 Reflections

This space is for you to make a note of things you have learnt in this unit. You can also use it as a diary to write about your problems and progress in English.

....
....
....
....
....
....
....
....
....

13

IT'S BETTER TO TRAVEL THAN TO ARRIVE

1 Verbs and phrases

Complete the sentences with a suitable verb. (They are all in Unit 13 of the Class Book.)

1. I found this pen on the floor. Does it .... to you?

2. If you don't take your own car you can .... one at the airport when you arrive. It's not expensive but remember to take your licence with you.

3. I'm leaving very early so I must .... my packing this evening.

4. You should .... travel insurance if you go abroad.

5. You have to .... your flight in advance if you plan to travel during August.

6. It's a good service to the centre of town and buses .... every ten minutes.

7. When I arrived I had to .... a form for immigration.

8. I'm sorry to .... you, but have you got the time, please?

9. He .... my passport but didn't ask me any questions.

10. Do I have to .... a visa to go to the United States?

2 Before leaving home ...

Look at these two possible constructions following *before* and *after*.

Examples: *Before* $\genfrac{}{}{0pt}{}{leaving}{I\ leave}$ *home I always check the doors.*

People often drink a lot after $\genfrac{}{}{0pt}{}{they\ play}{playing}$ *squash.*

Complete these sentences using *before* or *after* and a verb + *-ing*.

1. We must buy some souvenirs .... back home.

2. I felt terrible .... those chocolates.

3. She always puts on suntan lotion .... to the beach.

4. We had to take a taxi .... the bus.

5. I usually read in bed .... to sleep.

6. When you are driving you should always look in your mirror .... left or right.

7. .... the dinner for the family, I sat down and had a rest.

8. I must finish this exercise .... at the Answer Key.

3 I want some information

There is a mistake with an uncountable noun in each of these sentences.
Find the mistakes and correct them.

1. I asked her for an information.
2. We will need a lot of equipments.
3. How many luggage have you got?
4. It's a wonderful news.
5. He gave me some advices.
6. We had a wonderful weather.
7. Unfortunately I got a flu on holiday.
8. We had some troubles at the airport.

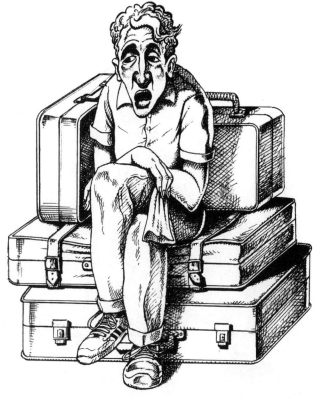

Listen carefully to the recording
and check your answers.

4 Sorry to bother you, but ...

Look again at the questions on page 86 in the Class Book. Write a question for each
of these answers.

Example: A: *Could I see your licence?* ....?

B: *Yes, of course. Here you are.*

1. A: ....?

   B: No, that's not mine. The bag I lost is bigger than that.

2. A: ....?

   B: Yes, of course. Just a minute, my wife has got the key.

3. A: ....?

   B: Yes, all cars are available immediately – they are parked just outside.

4. A: ....?

   B: Every ten minutes – it's an excellent service.

5. A: ....?

   B: Well, it's brown, made of leather, quite a big suitcase, in fact, and it's got my name and
   address on the label.

6. A: ....?

   B: Yes, sure – oh, do I really need to put my date of birth?

7. A: ....?

   B: Don't worry, madam. It will be very quick.

8. A: ....?

   B: Yes, of course. Could you give me the address where you are staying? And will you be at
   home in the evenings?

5 Travel tips from the Queen

She is one of the world's most experienced travellers, so find out what she does and underline anything which is true for you as well.

IT'S true that the Queen has an army of people to help her, but some of her travelling tips may still be useful for the rest of us.

Number one, the Queen is physically fit. She takes her dogs for regular walks, and at the weekend she rides and walks a great deal. She also has regular medical check-ups.

In hot climates especially, the Queen only eats very simple food, and she never overeats. At banquets, for example, she can give the impression that she is eating a lot, but in actual fact she may only have two or three mouthfuls.

She drinks very little alcohol and she never drinks local water. Everywhere she goes she takes bottled water with her, both for drinking in private, and cleaning her teeth.

The Queen only wears natural fibres – wool, silk, cotton – and all materials have to pass the 'crease test', which means that they do not need ironing all the time. Fortunately there are dressers who travel ahead of the Queen to unpack, but all her clothes travel in hanging wardrobes so that they arrive in perfect condition and do not need ironing.

Making certain her feet are comfortable is a priority for the Queen. She finds a style of shoe that is comfortable and then buys several pairs. For hot climates she has open-sided shoes and she changes her shoes several times a day to give her feet a rest.

It is important when travelling not to rush around or put your weight on one foot for too long. The Queen changes weight from one foot to the other to give each foot a rest, and she walks everywhere at a steady relaxed pace.

Finally, she tries to keep her normal sleep pattern, even when travelling abroad. That means that engagements are timed to finish at midnight, and when she is off-duty she prefers to be in bed by 11 o'clock. In the morning she is called at 7.30 with early-morning tea, just as at home. And she never takes a nap (a short sleep) during the day.

6 The last minute

What do you or your family do in the last five or ten minutes before leaving the house to go on holiday? Put a tick or cross in the table.

	You	Andrew	Patti
1. Check the windows are locked	....	....	....
2. Turn off the gas	....	....	....
3. Unplug all the electrical appliances	....	....	....
4. Say goodbye to your neighbour	....	....	....
5. Check your passport and tickets	....	....	....
6. Hide all your valuable things	....	....	....
7. Look in the rooms to make sure you haven't forgotten anything	....	....	....
8. Turn off the water	....	....	....
9. Draw the curtains	....	....	....
10. Go to the toilet	....	....	....

▭ Now listen to the recording and complete the table for Andrew and Patti.

7 Lovely to be here

A You and your friend are in the middle of a flight and you decide to write a postcard to someone in your group. Complete this one:

Dear ....,

We're on our way to .... for ...., and at the moment we're flying

over .... So far the journey has been .... The food is

.... and we've just seen .... – it's the in-flight movie. We are both

feeling a bit .... now, but fortunately we should arrive in about ....

See you in ....,

Yours,

.... and ....

B After a few days you decide to write another postcard. Complete this one:

........................,

We've been in .... for ...., and we're having

.... The weather is .... and we've been ....

several times. Yesterday we .... and tomorrow we're going

....

See you in ....

Best wishes,

.... and ....

PS Tell us if we've .... any mistakes.

8 Speaking partners

A Discuss your answers to Exercise 5, and then make a list together of travelling tips based on your own experience. For example, do you have a special method for making sure that nobody steals your money?

B Tell your partner about:

- the last journey you went on
- the best journey you've ever had
- the worst journey you've ever had
- your feelings about flying, long car journeys and long train journeys.

9 Visual dictionary

Complete the visual dictionary on page 126.

10 Reflections

This space is for you to make a note of things you have learnt in this unit. You can also use it as a diary to write about your problems and progress in English.

....

....

....

....

....

....

....

....

....

....

....

....

....

....

....

14

POSSESSIONS

With the present perfect tense, *for* + time expression describes the *period* during which something has or hasn't happened, or been true.

Example: *I've known her for a couple of years.*
I've known her for a very long time.
I've known her for six weeks.

Since + time expression indicates the *first or last time before now* that something has or hasn't happened. So *since* is used with a point in time.

Example: *I've had this car since last year.*
She hasn't been home since Thursday.

Divide these time expressions under two headings:
For and *Since*.
There are ten for
each heading.

six o'clock
last Tuesday
a week
two years
a couple of minutes
yesterday
the end of June
over a month
last November
three or four weeks
a century
December 12th
at least ten days
months and months
this morning
a little while
I wrote to you
mid August
I was 16
ages

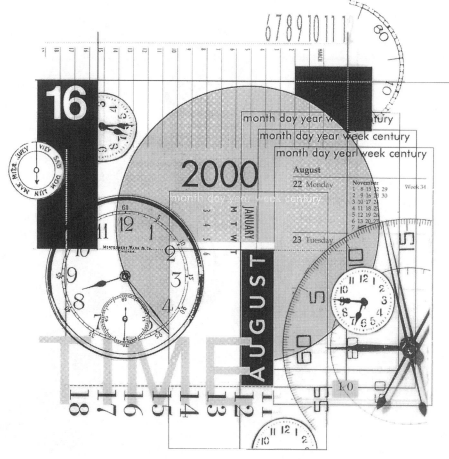

⫿⫾ Listen to the verbs on the recording. When you hear a verb, say the past participle in a sentence, like this:

Examples: *drive – I've driven it.*
wash – I've washed it.

You will hear the correct answer immediately after you speak so that you can check your grammar and pronunciation.

---

3 Bedside table and bedside lamp

Look at the compound nouns below. How many more compound nouns can you make with the underlined words? Use a dictionary to help you expand your vocabulary.

Example: <u>bedside</u> table   **bedside lamp**

<u>coffee</u> table ....

<u>book</u>case ....

<u>sports</u> car ....

<u>fire</u>place ....

<u>eye</u>brows ....

<u>french</u> windows ....

4 Electrical appliances

Match the words and pictures.

microwave oven
digital watch
video recorder
mobile phone
video camera
television with remote control
car radio/stereo
washing machine
clock radio
compact camera
calculator
computer
compact disc player

How many of these appliances do you use?
Write down the ones you use in the following columns:

Easy to use	Difficult or complicated to use
....	....
....	....
....	....
....	....
....	....
....	....

Do you use all the different features of your appliances?

5 Problems with electrical appliances

⬚ Listen to the recording and write down the problems in the table. Put a tick beside the problems you have yourself.

	Problem
Speaker 1	....
Speaker 2	....
Speaker 3	....
Speaker 4	....
Speaker 5	....
Speaker 6	....

6 High-tech appliances

Read the text and answer the questions at the end of each section.

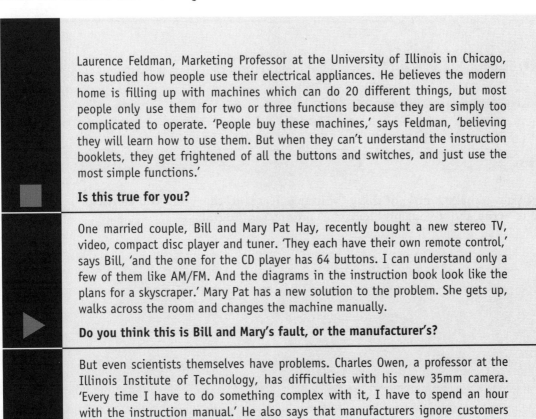

Laurence Feldman, Marketing Professor at the University of Illinois in Chicago, has studied how people use their electrical appliances. He believes the modern home is filling up with machines which can do 20 different things, but most people only use them for two or three functions because they are simply too complicated to operate. 'People buy these machines,' says Feldman, 'believing they will learn how to use them. But when they can't understand the instruction booklets, they get frightened of all the buttons and switches, and just use the most simple functions.'

Is this true for you?

One married couple, Bill and Mary Pat Hay, recently bought a new stereo TV, video, compact disc player and tuner. 'They each have their own remote control,' says Bill, 'and the one for the CD player has 64 buttons. I can understand only a few of them like AM/FM. And the diagrams in the instruction book look like the plans for a skyscraper.' Mary Pat has a new solution to the problem. She gets up, walks across the room and changes the machine manually.

Do you think this is Bill and Mary's fault, or the manufacturer's?

But even scientists themselves have problems. Charles Owen, a professor at the Illinois Institute of Technology, has difficulties with his new 35mm camera. 'Every time I have to do something complex with it, I have to spend an hour with the instruction manual.' He also says that manufacturers ignore customers and produce poor instruction manuals.

Have you ever had a poor instruction booklet?

People often buy these high-tech objects for status. Do they really need a video that can record 4 programmes over 21 days? If we continue to buy these appliances just because they look good, that's what manufacturers will sell us.

What do you think? Do you agree or disagree?

7 A description of a home

Read the description of a home on page 92 in your Class Book again. Then look at the picture of a home in your visual dictionary on page 127 and write a similar description. Use these phrases:

As you walk up the path, you come to …
You go into the hall and …
Moving on to the living room, …

8 Speaking partners

A Find an instruction manual for an appliance. If possible, find one which has a translation in English. Look at a simple instruction in your language. Try to translate it into English, and then see what the English translation says. Discuss it with your speaking partner.

B Look in your pockets, briefcase, handbag, etc. Make a list of everything you have got in English. Use a dictionary if necessary. Tell your speaking partner what you have, and teach them any words they didn't know.

C Do you sometimes have problems with electrical appliances? Tell your speaking partner.

9 Visual dictionary

Complete the visual dictionary on page 127.

10 Reflections

This space is for you to make a note of things you have learnt in this unit. You can also use it as a diary to write about your problems and progress in English.

15

RULES

1 Places

Match the words in the two boxes, and write them in a list, using an article if necessary.

Box 1

| Canary | Mount | Lake | Atlantic | Black | National | Atlas | River |

Box 2

| Mountains | Everest | Gallery | Islands | Nile | Constance | Ocean | Sea |

The Canary Islands ....

....

....

....

2 Obligation and permission

Rewrite the sentences (about a very strict hotel) beginning with the words you are given.

Example: *We had to have breakfast at 8 o'clock.*

We couldn't .have breakfast when we wanted. ....

1. We couldn't get a room without booking.

   We had to ....

2. We had to stay at least two nights.

   We couldn't ....

3. We couldn't use the car park at the front.

   We had to ....

4. We had to go to the dining room for all meals.

   We couldn't ....

   ....

5. Men couldn't wear open-necked shirts in the

   dining room.

   Men had to ....

   ....

6. When we left, we had to vacate the room by

   10.30 am.

   When we left, we couldn't ....

   ....

7. And we couldn't pay by credit card.

   We had to ....

   ....

But at least we don't have to go back there again!

---

3 Don't make a mistake

vocabulary: collocation

A Match words from Box A with words from Box B to form ten common expressions.

A				B		
	wait	blow			one's turn	the room
	kick	shake			a uniform	a letter
	leave	make			hands	an exam
	address	break			one's nose	a ball
	wear	take			a call	a rule

....

....

....

....

....

....

....

....

....

....

B Now cover the answers and complete these sentences with the correct verb.

1. I always .... hands when I meet people for the first time.

2. She asked the teacher if she could .... the room.

3. We had to .... a uniform at school.

4. I was in a hurry but I had to .... my turn in the shop.

5. I wanted to .... my nose but I didn't have a handkerchief.

6. My foot hurts when I .... the ball.

7. I had to .... an exam at the end of the course.

8. I didn't .... the letter correctly; that's why it didn't arrive.

9. Could I .... a quick call before we leave?

10. If you .... the rules, you get into trouble.

4 Right or wrong?
language rules

Look at these rules and decide if you think they are correct or not. If necessary, change them.

1. *Who* is normally only used to refer to people.

....

2. Days of the week and months of the year are always written with a capital letter.

....

3. The letter *k* at the beginning of a word is only pronounced if the next letter is *n*.

....

4. Some words which look plural in English are in fact used with singular verbs. (Examples: *mathematics, politics, news*.)

....

....

5. *Pleased to meet you* is a useful greeting when you meet someone for the first time in a formal situation.

....

....

6. If you are writing a letter to someone in English, it is normal to write your own address and the date in the top right-hand corner.

....

....

7. You cannot use the present continuous (example: *I'm working*) to talk about the future.

....

8. You use the infinitive with *to* after the verb *must*.

....

9. Nouns are always stressed on the first syllable.

....

5 Good and bad language rules
listening

▭ Listen to the recording and check your answers to Exercise 4. Make any necessary changes to the rules.

Look at the rules again. Which ones do *you* think are useful? Tell your speaking partner next time you see them.

The following passage is from *A Dictionary of Etiquette*, published in 1911. Read it and then go on to Exercise 7. (Underlined words are explained in the glossary at the side.)

Attentions from a gentleman to a lady

IF A LADY wishes to go further in her <u>acquaintance</u> with a gentleman she must make the first <u>advance</u>, and he must be ready at all times to meet such advances. If he meets the lady in the street, he should wait for her to bow and then take off his hat. If she stops to speak to him, he must never keep her standing, but must walk with her in the direction in which she is going. If he is riding at the time he must <u>dismount</u> and walk with her. The practice of walking arm in arm in the street is now <u>out of date</u>, but in a crowd it would be right for a gentleman to offer his arm to a lady, or go before her to clear the way for her.

A gentleman must always raise his hat when a lady bows to him, even if he does not remember who she is.

It is correct for a gentleman to stand up when a lady enters the room, and remain standing until she is seated. He must also stand up when she leaves the room, and should open the door for her. These rules should be observed whether the lady is known to the gentleman or not. A gentleman should follow a lady on going up or downstairs; but he must <u>precede her</u> on <u>alighting</u> from a carriage or public <u>vehicle</u>.

A gentleman does not force his attentions upon a lady. If she shows by her manner that his presence is not agreeable, he should <u>withdraw</u> at once. On the other hand, it is not etiquette for a gentleman to leave a lady <u>abruptly</u> just because she is bored with his company. He must wait for an opportunity to withdraw without hurting her feelings.

GLOSSARY

acquaintance (here) = the relationship

advance = contact

dismount = get off one's horse

out of date = old-fashioned; not common now

precede her = go before her

alighting = getting out (of the carriage)

vehicle = a general word for forms of road transport: cars, buses, and bicycles are all types of vehicle

withdraw (here) = go away (It also means to take out money from a bank account.)

abruptly = quickly and in a way which is quite rude

---

7 Expressing opinions   writing

Think about the rules you have just read, and then complete the following sentences, giving your own opinion.

I think men should still ....

....

I don't think men should still ....

....

I think women should ....

....

I don't think women should ....

....

8 Speaking partners

A If you are studying in your own country, look around you for examples of rules
written in your own language. For example: on buses, in shops, in hotels, in banks and
so on. Make a list of them and write down how you would explain these rules to
someone in English. Then compare them with your speaking partner.

If you are studying in an English-speaking country, keep a record of written rules that
you find, and try translating them into your own language. Show your speaking partner
the rules you have found and discuss them.
You could also compare your translations with someone who speaks the same
language. Here are some examples:

Please do not lean out of the window (In trains)
Please queue other side (In banks, post offices, at bus stops)
Keep off the grass (In some parks)
Do not leave bags unattended (In some public places, e.g. railway stations)

B Compare your answers to Exercise 7 above.

C Think about the rules you have in your conversations with your speaking partner.
For example:

1. Do you have a rule that you speak to each other at least once a week?
2. Do you have a rule that you cannot use your first language?
3. Do you have any rules at all?

Discuss the rules that you have. Are they good rules? Do you need some new ones?

9 Reflections

This space is for you to make a note of things you have learnt in this unit. You can also
use it as a diary to write about your problems and progress in English.

....

....

....

....

....

....

....

....

....

....

....

....

16

KEEPING THE CUSTOMER SATISFIED

1 If it rains ...

If sentences with will

A Match the two halves of the following sentences.

1. If it rains
2. If it bleeds
3. If the bank isn't open
4. If she speaks very quickly
5. If I don't pass the exam
6. If I see Catherine
7. If I get lost
8. If I miss the bus
9. If the music is very loud
10. If I win lots of money

a. I'll have to take it again.
b. I'll look on the map.
c. I won't understand.
d. I'll put a bandage on it.
e. I won't get there on time.
f. I'll tell them to turn it down.
g. I'll give her your regards.
h. I won't spend all of it.
i. I'll take an umbrella.
j. I'll deposit the money tomorrow.

B Now change each *if* clause from positive to negative, or negative to positive, and then complete each sentence in a logical way.

Examples: *If it doesn't rain,* ...I'll go for a walk............

If it doesn't bleed, ...I won't need a bandage............

2 Forming opposites

vocabulary: prefixes

Use these prefixes to form opposites of the words below.

| un- im- in- il- |

helpful *unhelpful*.........
efficient ....
friendly ....
polite ....
reliable ....
legal ....

employed ....
possible ....
experienced ....
logical ....
necessary ....
suitable ....

unhelpful

3 Syllables and word stress

pronunciation

A How many syllables are there in each of these words?

Examples: *cli-ent* (2)
em-ploy-er (3)
e-du-ca-tion (4)

opposite	message	Wednesday	experience	research	reliable
economist	polite	business	questionnaire	appearance	suitable
competition	vegetarian

B Now put the words into the correct column according to the main stress.

1st syllable	2nd syllable	3rd syllable
▢ client	▢ employer	▢ education
▢ opposite	....	....
....	....	....
....	....	....
....	....	....
....	....	....

⬚⬚ Listen and check your answers.

---

4 Synonyms and opposites in business

Replace the underlined word in these sentences with a word or phrase of similar meaning.

1. Ten <u>workers</u> lost their jobs.
2. Sales have <u>increased</u> this year.
3. The company is very <u>dependable</u>.
4. We have a lot of important <u>customers</u> in the Middle East.
5. I had to <u>withdraw</u> $1,000 from my account last week.

Now replace the underlined word in the sentences below with a word that has the opposite meaning.

6. I <u>bought</u> the car last week.
7. We made a small <u>profit</u> last year.
8. Sales have <u>risen</u> this month.
9. It's a very <u>reliable</u> company.
10. We may <u>get more</u> business if we <u>reduce</u> our prices.

---

5 Nouns formed with -ness

The suffix *-ness* combines with many adjectives to form nouns:

Examples: *dark – darkness*; *friendly – friendliness*
(Notice the change in spelling in the last example.)

In the following list of fifteen adjectives, twelve form nouns with *-ness*. Find the three words that do not, then complete the box.

Adjective	Noun	Adjective	Noun	Adjective	Noun
polite	....	warm	....	sad	....
happy	....	weak	....	stupid	....
ill	....	rude	....	lonely	....
efficient	....	sick	....	kind	....
mad	....	blind	....	helpful	....

Here are some predictions about life in Britain in 2010. Can you find two things you think *will* be true of your country, two things that *might* be true of your country, and two things that *won't* come true in your country?

Example: *I agree that the working week will be shorter, but I don't*
think that people will smoke less in my country.

POPULATION:

The population will increase by 3-4% to approximately 60 million, but the age spread will change dramatically:

Age	Change
2–24	down 14%
2–29	down 23%
30–34	down 17%
over 80	up 26%

Life expectancy for women will rise to 79.4 (in 1990 it was 78.2). For men it will increase to 74.3 (compared with 72.3 in 1990).

WORK:

A working week might be only three and a half days, and a typical worker will receive 15 weeks holiday a year. Retirement will also be earlier for most people - for some it might be as early as 50.

More people will work from home using computers, but it still won't be very common because most jobs can't be done from a distance.

FOOD AND DRINK:

We will buy more expensive food but we will still spend less of our income on it. Our diets will change quite considerably:

–less meat, milk, cheese, eggs and butter;
–more fish, fruit, vegetables and manufactured foods.

Our drinking and smoking habits will change as well. Beer consumption will go down by 20%, but wine consumption will go up by 60%. Sales of tobacco will go down by 40%.

CLOTHES AND SHOPPING:

We will spend much more on our clothes and appearance, e.g. 49% more on cosmetics and 36% more on jewellery and watches. Surprisingly, we will spend the same amount on hairdressing.

The biggest change in shopping will be the location. Shops will get bigger and bigger, and many of them will be located outside of town. People will also shop from home, but the desire to see and touch things will mean that some people will still prefer to visit shops.

LEISURE:

In 2010 we will probably watch the same amount of TV, but there will be many more channels to choose from. The greatest changes will be in foreign travel, which will go up by 157%; the sale of sports equipment, which will rise by 116%; and eating out, which will go up by 99%.

□□ Listen to the woman on the recording talking about the future. What does she say about the following?

1. population *She thinks it might rise.* ....

2. a. life expectancy for women ....

   b. life expectancy for men ....

3. age of retirement ....

4. diet ....

5. money we spend on clothes ....

6. shops ....

7. leisure ....

8. foreign travel ....

9. eating out ....

There are many fixed phrases used in business letters. Here are some:

Enquiry

I am writing to enquire about ...

or

I am interested in ...

I would be grateful if you could send ...

or

Could you possibly send ...

I look forward to hearing from you.

Reply

Thank you for your letter of 25 May, requesting details of ...

I am enclosing ...

or

Please find enclosed ...

If you require any further information, please do not hesitate to contact me.

or

We look forward to hearing from you.

John Patterson wrote a letter of enquiry to Sunland Furnishings. This is the reply he received. Read it, then write the letter of enquiry John Patterson wrote on 28 May.

Sunland Furnishings
East Street Sunleigh Essex

Mr J Patterson
3 Acacia Avenue
London N5

30 May 1995

Dear Mr Patterson

Thank you for your letter of 28 May, requesting details of our new 'Summer Shade' range of garden furniture.

I am enclosing a copy of our current brochure, and I should like to draw your attention to the quantity discounts on page 15. If you decide to purchase any items from the new range, we can also arrange for delivery in the UK mainland within 28 days, free of charge.

We look forward to hearing from you.

Your sincerely

Martin Turner

Martin Turner
Sales Manager

3 Acacia Avenue
London N5

The Manager
Sunland Furnishings
East Street
Sunleigh
Essex

28 May 1995

Notice that:

1. It is now standard in typed business letters to omit commas after *Dear Sir* and *Yours sincerely*. There is also no punctuation in the address and the date is simply 28 May (not 28th).
2. Each paragraph begins at the left-hand margin, and there is a space between each paragraph.
3. If you begin a letter with the name, you finish with *Yours sincerely*. If you begin a letter *Dear Sir* or *Dear Madam*, you normally end *Yours faithfully* in British English.

9 Speaking partners

A Compare the predictions you made in Exercise 6.

B Have you ever worked in a situation where you had customers? If so, tell your speaking partner about it.

- Where were you working?
- What were the customers like?
- Did you ever have any problems with them? If so, what?

10 Reflections

This space is for you to make a note of things you have learnt in this unit. You can also use it as a diary to write about your problems and progress in English.

....
....
....
....
....
....

17

PICTURE THIS!

1 Logical endings

Complete these sentences in a logical way.

1. I bought a dictionary so that ....

2. He does a lot of overtime so that ....

3. She got up early so that ....

4. I always go to the supermarket on Friday so that ....

5. We must go now, otherwise ....

6. Take an umbrella, otherwise ....

7. She must work hard, otherwise ....

8. Write down new words in your notebook, otherwise ....

2 Put them in order

You are giving advice to someone who is coming to your country for a holiday. Make complete sentences from these jumbled words.

1. learn   ~~of~~   a   ~~first~~   try   language   few   ~~all~~   to   words   our   in

   First of all, ...

2. good   sure   you   book   secondly   buy   make   a   guide

   ....

3. to   usual   try   the   places   thirdly   tourist   avoid

   ....

4. forget   finally   phone   you   to   arrive   when   don't   me

   ....

3 Word partnerships

A Complete the phrases with words from the box.

make ....

do ....

....

....

....

....

tell ....

take ....

....

....

....

....

the shopping   a mistake   a photo   a story   the truth   someone a favour   homework   a lie   an appointment   a taxi   a noise   a shower

B Without looking at Part A, fill the first gaps in each of these sentences with the correct verb.

In my opinion:

1. People who always .... mistakes are ....

2. People who always .... the truth are ....

3. People who always .... taxis are ....

4. People who .... lies are ....

5. People who .... appointments and then break them are ....

6. People who always .... a lot of noise are ....

7. People who .... amusing stories are ....

8. People who never .... anyone a favour are ....

C ⊂⊃ Now finish each of the sentences using an adjective from the following box (use a dictionary to help you), and then listen to the speaker completing the same sentences on the recording.

funny   honest   irritating   lazy   careless   mean   dishonest   unreliable

4 Wordsearch

There are ten words in the word square from Unit 17 in the Class Book. Can you find them? They can be up, down, diagonal, backwards and forwards.

⇧ ⇩ ⬈ ⬊ ⇦ ⇨

```
E S O O H C A E P T
V P S E L B P T A I
I M F O X C A I N S
S O S R L L R F I Y
S E D N W K R D C B
E L K J Y Z O R U A
R E C E I P T B V B
G I C N M E P H G G
G E V D N T J A O H
A V O I D P E K O J
```

Read this poem with a dictionary. Then listen to the recording and fill in the gaps.

a hot spring day by the lake
and a young woman and man
probably tourists
possibly ....
who wanted a photo of themselves ....
handed their camera to someone

almost definitely ....
who certain fellow countrymen
might predictably describe
as a very drunken old dosser*
but to them he was just a ....
he accepted the camera
took a long time focusing

and steadying himself
but managed to take the ....
and received genuine gratitude
from the two
who had seen nothing deviant in his behaviour
and who would remember him

as a friendly and ....
English ....
if he hadn't fallen into the lake
with their ....

John Hegley

* a person who lives on the streets (slang)

A Rosa is going to lend her camera to her younger brother, Bernie. Read the letter she sent him with the camera.

> 17 Blewton Street
> Cambridge
>
> 17th September
>
> Dear Bernie,
>   As I promised, here's my camera. It's not difficult to use but I would just like to give you a few words of advice.
>   First of all, don't forget that it uses up batteries very quickly, so please be sure you turn it off when you aren't using it. And if you need to change the batteries, remember to get lithium ones.
>   Secondly, could you try and remember to keep it in the carrying case- especially if you take it to the beach.
>   And one last thing. Please don't forget to return it as soon as you get home because I'll need it for Julia's wedding on the 10th.
>   Anyway, have a lovely holiday and I hope you take some great photos.
>
>   Love,
>   Rosa

Notice that:

a. Rosa writes her address in the top right-hand corner. This is common to all letters.
b. Rosa also writes the date under the address. You can do this in several ways: *17 September* (common now in formal business letters), or *17th September*, or *September 17th*, or *17-9-95*.
c. She begins the letter *Dear ...* . We do this in all letters.
d. She finishes her letter *Love, ...* . This is normal when you write to your family or close friends (but not usually used by men writing to male friends). To other friends we normally put *Best wishes*, and in formal letters we use *Yours sincerely*, or *Yours faithfully*.

B You are going to lend a friend one of the following:

| your bike | your personal stereo | your portable computer |

Write a letter similar to Rosa's, and try to include some of the phrases from her letter. If you want, you could show the letter to your teacher or your speaking partner.

7 Speaking partners

A Before you meet your partner, find two or three photos to take with you of yourself, your family or your friends. When you meet, tell each other about your photos.

Here are some possible questions:

Who took the photos?
Where?
When?
Why?
Who are the people?
What kind of camera did you use?

Talk about how people look in the photos.

B If you have a camera, have a look at the instruction manual. Is the text in English and in your language? If so, translate some of the English text, and check it against the text written in your own language.

You could also do this with the instructions which come with camera film.

C Before you meet your partner, think about a problem you have at the moment that you feel happy to discuss with them. Ask them to give you some advice.

8 Visual dictionary

Complete the visual dictionary on page 128.

9 Reflections

This space is for you to make a note of things you have learnt in this unit. You can also use it as a diary to write about your problems and progress in English.

....

....

....

....

....

....

....

....

....

18

LISTS

1 Could you lend me some money?

A Check you understand the words in the box. Use a dictionary if necessary.

> an apology   an invitation
> thanks   a plan   a request
> advice   an excuse
> a suggestion

Would you like to go out this evening?

I can't – I'm not free.

The sentences below are examples
of the words in the box.
Can you match them correctly?

Example: *I'm going to Jamaica for my holiday this year.*   **a plan**

1. Would you like to go out this evening? ....

   ....

2. How about next Tuesday? ....

   ....

3. Could you lend me some money? ....

   ....

4. I think you should phone the police. ....

   ....

5. I'm sorry I'm late. ....

   ....

6. Oh, that's very kind of you. ....

   ....

7. I intend to start a new business next year. ....

   ....

8. I'm late because the traffic was terrible. ....

   ....

B Think of a positive response to each of the above situations, and write your answers
in the spaces provided.

Example: A: *I'm going to Jamaica for my holiday this year.*
         B: *Really? That'll be lovely.*

⟳ Now listen to the replies on the recording and compare them with your own.

2 On the telephone

Correct the errors in these telephone conversations.

1. A: Hello?
   B: Are you John?
   A: Yes, I am.
   B: Oh, hello, John, here is Hans.

2. A: Good morning, Reebok.
   B: Good morning. I want speak with Mr Graham.
   A: Yes, who's calling, please?
   B: I am Maria Selbeck.
   A: Right, one moment. I'll put you through.

3. A: Hello?
   B: Oh, I like speak to Jasna.
   A: I'm sorry, she's out. Can I take a message?
   B: No, it's OK. I ring back later.

4. A: Hello?
   B: Oh, hello, Catherine; it's Brian. How do you do?
   A: Thanks, fine. And you?
   B: Yes, I'm very fine too.

3 Lexical sets

A The following sentences all include lists, but one item in each list is missing. What could the missing item be?

1. He told me just to bring a knife, ... and spoon.

2. She was wearing flat shoes, a brown skirt and a white ....

3. You can get these jackets in cotton, suede or ....

4. They only sell three sizes: small, ... or large.

5. The hotel said they could provide bed and breakfast, half board or ....

6. It's a fixed-price menu, and you get a starter, a .... and a dessert.

7. They ask people not to smoke cigarettes, pipes or ....

8. It was a fairly typical bathroom: a bath, shower, toilet and ....

9. She won three medals at the Olympics: a gold, a .... and a bronze.

10. I had the hearts, and she had the clubs, spades and ....

B ⏏ Listen to the answers on the recording and write down any that are different from your own.

4 Intonation in lists

⏏ Listen to the answers to Exercise 3 again, and notice the intonation of the speaker when she reads a list:

Example: *He told me just to bring a knife, fork and spoon.*

Using the same intonation, practise saying the sentences yourself. If possible, do it with your speaking partner, or record your sentences onto a cassette and then listen to them.

5 Complete the phrase

Complete these sentences with common fixed phrases.

1. A: Have you got the time?

   B: No, I'm ....

2. A: Are you going to the party tonight?

   B: No, I don't ....

3. A: I'm sorry, I've forgotten your book.

   B: .... It's not important.

4. Everyone came last night .... Jill. She was ill.

5. A: Did he go with friends?

   B: No, he went ....

6. I went by bus, but the others went .... so it took them a lot longer.

7. I don't know how many there were, but .... 20, I'm sure.

8. A: When do you want to meet?

   B: I don't know. .... next Tuesday?

9. A: Shall I carry that for you?

   B: Oh, ... Thank you.

10. A: How are you?

    B: .... And you?

6 Memory aids

Making lists is one method that people use to remember things. Here are some others. Read the text and think which of them you use yourself.

1. A diary
2. Rhymes. For example, 'In fourteen hundred and ninety-*two*, Columbus sailed the ocean *blue*' helps you to remember 1492.
3. Writing on one's hand (or some other part of the body).
4. The story method. You make up a story which connects the items to be remembered in the right order.
5. First letter memory aids. For example, the first letters of 'Richard Of York Gave Battle In Vain' give you the first letters of the colours of the rainbow (red, orange, yellow, green, blue, indigo, violet).
6. Alphabetical searching. You go through the letters of the alphabet one after another to try to remember the first letter of a name or something.
7. Memos. For example, writing notes to yourself and lists of things to do.
8. Calendars and year planners.
9. The place method. With this method, the things you must remember are imagined in familiar places. Looking in these places then reminds you of the things you had to remember.

10. Asking other people to remember things for you and remind you about them.
11. Leaving objects in special or unusual places. This helps you to remember where they are.
12. Alarm clocks, watches, telephones, calculators, etc., which you can use to help you remember things. For example, you have to phone someone at three o'clock, so you set your alarm clock for three o'clock.
13. Going back through a sequence of events. People sometimes go back through a series of events in their minds in order to remember when something happened.

Which method would be helpful to remember the following things?

a. A friend's birthday.
b. Where you left your glasses.
c. The name of a famous film star. You know the name but just at this moment you can't remember it.
d. Someone's telephone number, and also to remember to phone them from your office this afternoon. (It is now the morning and you are at home.)
e. You have to put some meat in the oven at four thirty this afternoon (it is now two o'clock).
f. You have just bought six items of clothing from six different shops, and you want to remember where you bought everything because a friend may want to know.

---

7 A list of facts

listening

▭ Listen and complete the following list:

Date	Craft	Time
1519–21	*Vittoria* (sailing ship)	2 years
....	USS *Triton* (..........................)	....
....	*Graf Zeppelin* (..........................)	....
....	*Chicago* (..........................)	....
....	USAF Boeing B–52	....
....	*Cosmos 169* (..........................)	....

What is this list? If you don't know, you will find the answer on page 151.

---

8 Language learning

writing

Choose two or three sentence beginnings from the following, and complete each one with 15–30 words. Then compare your sentences with those in the Answer Key.

I often make lists because ....
....

I never make lists because ....
....

I keep a record of vocabulary in this way: ....
....

I translate words into my own language when ....
....

I prefer a monolingual dictionary because ....
....

I prefer a bilingual dictionary because ....
....

Working with my speaking partner is ....
....

Speaking on the telephone in English is ....
....

9 Speaking partners

During the next few weeks try to make as many lists as you can in English. For example, when you go shopping, write a shopping list in English; when you have lots of things to do during the day/weekend/week, write them down in a list in English. Try to make lists at work as well. Compare your lists with your speaking partner.

10 Visual dictionary

Complete the visual dictionary on page 129.

11 Reflections

This space is for you to make a note of things you have learnt in this unit. You can also use it as a diary to write about your problems and progress in English.

....
....
....
....
....
....
....
....
....
....
....
....
....
....
....

19

PUT YOUR TRUST IN OTHERS

1 Correct the mistakes

Correct the errors in these sentences. Be careful: three of the sentences are correct.

1. What will you do if it rain tomorrow?
2. If I had a lot of money, I might decide to give up my job.
3. If he would lose his job, it would be terrible for the family.
4. We don't know what to say if she refused to help us this evening.
5. We have a great time if you come to the restaurant with us.
6. If she offered me a lift home, I would accept it.
7. I'll be astonished if you don't pass the test.
8. If somebody breaks into your flat tonight, what would you do?
9. If she will get the job, we'll be delighted.
10. I would complained if a restaurant served me bad food.

2 Just imagine

Rewrite these sentences using *would* or *wouldn't*.

Example: *I don't like football, so I'm not going to the match.*
          If I liked football, I would go to the match.

1. I live near the centre, so I don't need a car.

   If ....

2. I don't work on Saturdays, so I go to bed very late on Fridays.

   If ....

3. I have a big dog and I get lots of exercise.

   If ....

4. I don't eat at home often, so I don't need a dishwasher.

   If ....

5. I don't drink coffee at night because it keeps me awake.

   If ....

6. I don't understand the financial pages, so I don't read them.

If ....

7. The tickets are very expensive, so we're not going.

If ....

8. We have a babysitter, so we can go out.

If ....

3 From verb to noun

A Complete the table,
using a dictionary if necessary.

Verb	Noun
to explain	*explanation*
to refuse	
to accept	
to believe	
to invite	
to complain	
to offer	
to agree	

B Cover the table above, then complete these sentences with suitable nouns or verbs.

1. Did he send you an .... to his party?

2. I asked her to help me but she ....

3. She wrote a letter of .... to the manager about the poor service.

4. Did you understand the teacher's ....? I thought it was very clear.

5. Someone .... me $200 for my watch.

6. Do you .... his story? I don't think it can be true.

7. Excuse me, do you .... credit cards?

8. The two presidents signed a historic .... between their two countries.

4 I'm very boring!

Underline the correct adjective in these sentences.

1. It was a terrible film and I was very *boring/bored*.
2. I found the book very *depressing/depressed*.
3. It was very *embarrassing/embarrassed* when he made that comment about her dress.
4. We were quite *surprising/surprised* when she won the game.
5. Don't go to that restaurant – the food's *disgusting/disgusted*.
6. She looked very ill, and we were quite *shocking/shocked*.
7. I'm not *interesting/interested* in sport.
8. We were *frightening/frightened* when we heard that noise.
9. I thought the book was *boring/bored*.
10. I always get *depressing/depressed* when I watch the news on television.

Try to guess the meaning of the underlined words and phrases *as they appear in the story*.
Write down a translation for each one, and then at the end check in a bilingual
dictionary.

There was a young couple who lived on a new housing estate. They were <u>proud</u> of their
house and their car, which they kept in <u>immaculate</u> condition. They both took the same train
to work every morning, leaving the car parked outside their house. One morning they
opened the front door and ... their car was missing. They were very <u>upset</u> and they <u>rushed</u>
down to the police station to report the <u>theft</u>. The police took all the details and were very
sympathetic, but not very optimistic about getting the car back.

When the couple <u>eventually</u> returned home
from work that evening, they had a <u>miserable</u>
<u>supper</u> and went to bed. The next morning they
stepped outside their house and ... the car was
back. They were <u>astonished</u>. They walked all
round it, looking carefully – not a <u>scratch</u>. But
what was this? There was something on the front
seat. It was a bottle of champagne and a letter. 'I
am sorry I had to borrow your car,' it read. 'I am
a doctor and it was an emergency. Please accept
this bottle of champagne and these two tickets for
the theatre as a token of my appreciation.'

The couple were <u>delighted</u>. They phoned the
police and told them the story, and that night
they got dressed up and went to the theatre. They
had a great time, but as they were walking along
the road back to their house, they suddenly felt
<u>uneasy</u>. They ran to the house, but then <u>breathed</u>
<u>a sigh of relief</u>. The car was still there. They
opened the front door and went in. The house
was almost empty. Someone had broken in and
stolen just about everything – someone who
knew they would be out all evening.

Match the two halves of the sentences.

1. Parents feel proud when
2. A lot of people are miserable when
3. You can get soaked when
4. It's important to be optimistic when
5. Actors are always delighted when
6. Nurses try to be gentle when
7. I try not to get upset when
8. My boss is never sympathetic when
9. I'm always astonished when
10. You have to be tolerant when

a. they don't feel very well.
b. it rains heavily.
c. their patients are very sick.
d. your children are growing up.
e. my homework is all correct.
f. I get to work late because of traffic jams.
g. they get nice letters from fans.
h. my boss gets angry.
i. their children do well at school.
j. everything around you looks bad.

7 Offers and requests

📖 Listen and write down the sentences. Compare your answers with the tapescript on page 137.

8 Conditional sentences

A Do you have a car? If so, imagine you didn't, and write three consequences.

If I didn't have a car, ...

....

....

If you don't have a car, imagine that you did, and write three consequences.

If I had a car, ...

....

....

B Are you married? If so, imagine that you weren't, and write three consequences.

If I weren't married, ...

....

....

If not, imagine that you were, and write three consequences.

If I were married, ...

....

....

C Do you have a job? If so, imagine you didn't, and write three consequences.

If I didn't have a job, ...

....

....

If not, imagine that you did, and write three consequences.

If I had a job, ...

....

....

9 Speaking partners

A Read the story in Exercise 5 again and discuss these statements with your speaking partner.

1. The young couple were unlucky.
2. The person who took their car was a doctor.
3. The couple were stupid to believe the story in the letter.
4. The person who took their car probably broke into their house.
5. It's very common to get your car back if someone steals it.
6. This is not a true story.

B Show your partner your answers to the writing activity in Exercise 8. Can you add two more consequences to each other's lists?

C Look at these warning notices. Where would you see each one? Discuss with your speaking partner. If you both speak the same language, translate them together.

Do not leave parcels or bags unattended.

Do not leave valuables in your room. Please deposit them in the hotel safe.

Beware of pickpockets.

The management cannot accept any responsibility for valuables lost or stolen.

WATCH OUT!
THERE'S A THIEF ABOUT

Look after your luggage at all times.

10 Reflections

This space is for you to make a note of things you have learnt in this unit. You can also use it as a diary to write about your problems and progress in English.

....
....
....
....
....
....
....
....
....
....
....
....
....
....

20

THE SENSES

1 Agreeing

Look at these examples:

A: *I **work** in a bank.*
B: *So **do** I.*
(Use *so* because the sentence is positive.)

A: *I **don't use** the bus service.*
B: *Neither **do** I.*
(Use *neither* because the sentence is negative.)

We use this construction to show that we agree with someone, or that the information about us is the same. The auxiliary verb in the first speaker's statement is repeated in the answer.

Look at these examples using different verbs:

A: *I **can** hear birds singing.*
B: *So **can** I.*

A: *I **can't** swim.*
B: *Neither **can** I.*

A: *I'm leaving tomorrow.*
B: *So **am** I.*

A: *I'm not very busy.*
B: *Neither **am** I.*

Agree with the following statements.

1. I can't fly. _Neither can I._
2. I hate the smell of gas. ....
3. I don't live in a tent. ....
4. I can speak some English. ....
5. I like the sunshine. ....
6. I'm studying English. ....
7. I'm not going on holiday tomorrow. ....
8. I can't remember all the words I learnt yesterday. ....
9. I work quite hard. ....
10. I'm meeting someone next week. ....

2 Find the first letter

Complete the sentences by adding the first letter to each word.

1. I'm _ot _ure, _ut I _hink _t _ight _ain _gain _onight.
2. _o _ou _hink _here _ill _e _eople _iving _n _he _oon _n _wenty _ears' _ime?
3. _he's _ure _he _on't _ass _er _xams _ecause _he _asn't _orked _ard _nough.
4. _he _octor _hinks _e'll _ecover _uickly _rom _he _peration.
5. I _on't _hink _ur _eacher _ill _e _nnoyed _f _e _orget _o _o _ur _omework.
6. _'m _bsolutely _ertain _y _ister _ill _e _ate. _he _lways _s.

A Combine words from the two circles to make nine compound nouns.

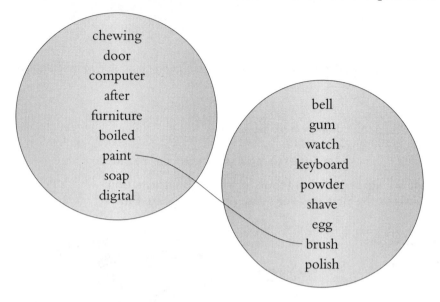

B Which word from above goes with each of these definitions?

1. Something you use to decorate the house. _paint brush_

2. This tells you the time. ....

3. Something you eat but don't swallow. ....

4. Something from a chicken which is then cooked. ....

5. Something you use to get your clothes clean. ....

6. Something you use to clean wooden tables and chairs. ....

7. Something men use on their faces. ....

8. Something to type on. ....

9. Something that tells you that you have visitors. ....

4 Listen and answer

vocabulary

▭ Write down your answers as you listen and then check with the tapescript on page 137.

5 Odd one out

pronunciation

Look at the underlined letters in these groups of words. How are they pronounced?
Which is the odd one out in each case?

Example: _grass_ _marble_ (_stamp_) _garlic_

1. sn<u>a</u>ke   ban<u>a</u>na   f<u>a</u>vourite   t<u>a</u>ste
2. h<u>o</u>ney   m<u>u</u>d   l<u>o</u>vely   nyl<u>o</u>n
3. sp<u>ea</u>k   l<u>ea</u>ther   pl<u>ea</u>sant   inst<u>ea</u>d
4. l<u>a</u>mb   s<u>a</u>lmon   or<u>a</u>nge   s<u>a</u>nd
5. f<u>o</u>rest   str<u>o</u>ng   c<u>o</u>tton   sm<u>o</u>ke
6. w<u>or</u>se   N<u>or</u>way   b<u>ur</u>n   f<u>ur</u>

▭ Listen to the recording to check your answers.

The senses are very often described at the beginning of a story to help the reader imagine the scene quickly. Read the beginning of this short story and then do the task below.

> THERE were about forty people at Jerry and Samantha's cocktail party that evening. It was the usual crowd, the usual discomfort, the usual appalling noise. People had to stand very close to one another and shout to make themselves heard. Many were grinning, showing capped, white teeth. Most of them had a cigarette in the left hand, a drink in the right.
>
> I moved away from my wife Mary and her group. I headed for the small bar in the far corner, and when I got there, I sat down on a bar stool and faced the room. I did this so that I could look at the women. I settled back with my shoulders against the bar-rail, sipping my Scotch.

Complete the sentences about the person in the story, like this:

He can hear **people talking to each other.**

He can see   ....

He can taste ....

He can smell ....

He can feel   ....

Add two more sounds, smells or sights to the scene.

Examples: *He can probably smell various perfumes that people are wearing.*
            He can probably hear some music in the background.

Compare your ideas with the suggestions on page 153.

CD Listen to the recording, and follow the instructions.

We arrived at ....

....

....

....

....

....

....

....

....

....

....

....

....

....

....

....

....

---

8 Speaking partners

A When you meet your partner, discuss these questions.

1. What are your two favourite smells? Do you know why?
2. Which is your favourite view in the place where you live? Can you describe it? Why do you like it so much?
3. Which sounds do you find frightening? Why?
4. Is there anything you hate touching? Do you know why?
5. Which tastes do you like most? Do you know why?

B Compare your answers to Exercise 6, and tell your partner the story you wrote in Exercise 7.

9 Visual dictionary

The picture on page 130 illustrates a number of nouns and verbs from the unit. How many can you identify?

10 Reflections

This space is for you to make a note of things you have learnt in this unit. You can also use it as a diary to write about your problems and progress in English.

21

TIME

Complete the sentences in a logical way using *used to*. Look at the example first.

Example: *It's a busy place now, but* ...*it used to be very quiet.*............

1. I'm retired now,

   but ....

2. I've got contact lenses now,

   but ....

3. I go jogging every day, so I'm quite fit,

   but ....

4. I think I'm quite self-confident now,

   but ....

5. I get on very well with my sister now,

   but ....

6. Car engines are very complicated these days,

   but ....

7. I really like studying English now,

   but ....

8. I spend a lot of time at home these days,

   but ....

Read these puzzles, then write numbers in the answer spaces.

Example: *eighty-three multiplied by six =* ...*498*.........

1. Six hundred and eighty-five plus two hundred and seven ....

2. The last date in April, June and November added together ....

3. Subtract the number of days in January from the number of days in an

   ordinary year. ....

4. Subtract the number of days in a week from the year the Second World War ended.

   ....

5. Imagine the year is fourteen ninety-two. What would be the year before last? ....

6. It's December the eighteenth, nineteen ninety-nine. What will the date be in a

   fortnight's time? ....

7. The year is eighteen eighteen. Subtract a couple of centuries, then add on a decade.

   ....

8. The number of units in this book divided by two. How many? ....

3 Saw or have seen?

Put either *I haven't seen her* or *I saw her* in front of the time expressions below. Look at the Grammar Reference on page 166 in the Class Book if you need help.

1. two weeks ago   *I saw her two weeks ago.*
2. this week   *I haven't seen her this week.*
3. last night   ....
4. since Tuesday   ....
5. in August   ....
6. yesterday   ....
7. in the last three weeks ....
8. yet   ....
9. before you came in   ....
10. at six o'clock   ....
11. this month   ....
12. when I was in Rome   ....
13. since I arrived   ....
14. ten years ago   ....
15. since last year   ....

4 At three o'clock in the morning

Learn this rule for the use of time prepositions.

at a time	e.g. at 3 o'clock; at 6.30 pm; at midnight
on a day	e.g. on Monday; on July 17th; on my birthday
in a period	e.g. in the morning; in January; in the summer; in 1992
Exceptions	at night; at Christmas; at Easter; at the weekend

Using different time expressions, complete the following sentences about yourself.

1. I was born ....
2. I started school ....
3. I usually go on holiday ....
4. I always clean my teeth ....
5. I usually leave the house in the morning ....
6. I sometimes go to parties ....
7. I sometimes go for long walks ....
8. My last lesson was ....
9. I take my clothes off ....
10. We have a national holiday ....

Unit 21 TIME

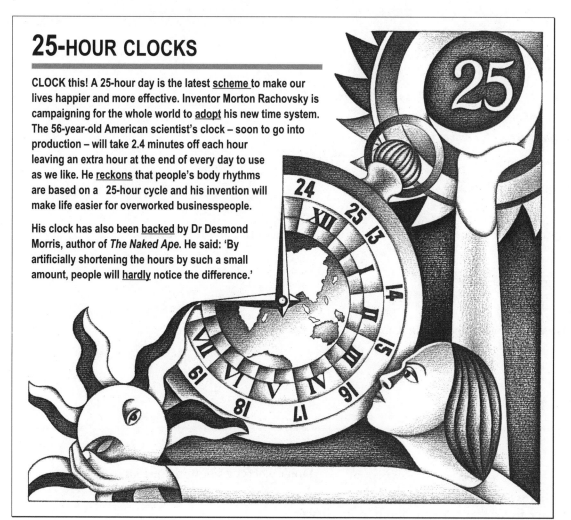

Listen to two people answering the same questions on the recording. Write down their answers in the box below.

	Woman		*Man*
1.	....		....
2.	....		....
3.	....		....
4.	....		....
5.	....		....
6.	....		....
7.	....		....
8.	....		....
9.	....		....
10.	....		....

5 Contextual guesswork

reading and vocabulary

Here is another text about time. While you read, try to think of words or phrases that you could use instead of the underlined words in the text.

25-HOUR CLOCKS

CLOCK this! A 25-hour day is the latest underline{scheme} to make our lives happier and more effective. Inventor Morton Rachovsky is campaigning for the whole world to underline{adopt} his new time system. The 56-year-old American scientist's clock – soon to go into production – will take 2.4 minutes off each hour leaving an extra hour at the end of every day to use as we like. He underline{reckons} that people's body rhythms are based on a 25-hour cycle and his invention will make life easier for overworked businesspeople.

His clock has also been underline{backed} by Dr Desmond Morris, author of *The Naked Ape*. He said: 'By artificially shortening the hours by such a small amount, people will underline{hardly} notice the difference.'

6 A time for everything

Here are two poems and a song all about time. Which do you know? Which do you like?

1.

The Clock on the Wall

My city collapsed
The clock was still on the wall
Our neighbourhood collapsed
The clock was still on the wall
The street collapsed
The clock was still on the wall
The square collapsed
The clock was still on the wall
The wall collapsed
The clock
Ticked on

Samih Al-Qasim

2.

Everything Changes
after Brecht, 'Alles wandelt sich'

Everything changes. We plant
trees for those born later
but what's happened has happened,
and poisons poured into the seas
cannot be drained out again.

What's happened has happened.
Poisons poured into the seas
cannot be drained out again, but
everything changes. We plant
trees for those born later.

Cicely Herbert

3.

To everything, turn, turn, turn,
There is a season, turn, turn, turn,
And a time for every purpose under
heaven.
A time to be born, a time to die,
A time to plant, a time to reap,
A time to kill, a time to heal,
A time to laugh, a time to weep.

Pete Seeger

7 How do you spend your time?

Listen and answer the questions. If you do not understand any, play the recording again.

8 Messages

Complete these messages in a suitable way.

Example:

Mary called. She'll be at work till ...quite late this evening.............................
because ..she has to finish a report for tomorrow.......
Could you ..get something for dinner tonight?.................

1. John rang while you ....

   Could you ring him before ....

   He ....

2. Mr Bassett wants you to contact him when .... because

   ....

3. Maria says she won't be back until ....

   so she's sorry but ....

4. A parcel arrived for you this morning. Can you come and collect it whenever

   ....? It looks

   ....

5. Your mother phoned while ....

   She said she ....

6. Phone the hospital as soon as ....

   It's about .... Don't worry; it's nothing serious.

Compare your answers with those suggested in the Answer Key. You can always check with your teacher if you are not sure about your answers.

9 Speaking partners

A What do you know about different times in your home town and country? Answer these questions together.

1. What are the opening and closing times of the following:
   banks? post offices? department stores? bars? chemists?
2. When do the following normally start and finish:
   schools? cinemas? theatres? parties?
3. What are the dates of national holidays?
4. What time do buses and trains start running in your home town?
5. When are the earliest and latest programmes on TV?

B You need a watch to time the exercise below. See how long it takes your partner to do these things, and write the time in the column on the right. Take it in turns to do a question.

Activity	Time taken
1. Count from 20 to 1 in English.	....
2. Say the alphabet in English.	....
3. Say ten irregular verbs in all forms.	....
e.g. *take–took–taken*	
4. Say the months of the year backwards – starting with the last month of the year.	....
5. Say the days of the week backwards – starting with the last day of the week.	....
6. Name ten objects you can both see now.	....
7. Name five jobs where you need to be able to speak in public.	....
8. Name five things you can buy at a stationer's.	....
9. Say five things you enjoy doing in your free time.	....
10. Say five things that you spend most of your life doing.	....

Who was quickest at each question? How much quicker can you answer all the questions in your own language?

10 Reflections

This space is for you to make a note of things you have learnt in this unit. You can also use it as a diary to write about your problems and progress in English.

....

....

....

....

....

....

....

....

....

22

A SENSE OF HISTORY

1 He was arrested outside the bank

A Look at the passive constructions below. Next to each one, write *present passive* or *past passive* or *future passive*.

He **was arrested** outside the bank. ....

The job **will be finished** by the weekend. ....

The play **is based** on a story by Tolstoy. ....

They **were sent** to prison. ....

The cars **are made** in Sweden. ....

The books **will be published** next year. ....

B Complete the following sentences using passive constructions. The verbs you need are all in the box at the end.

1. She .... to hospital last week. She .... blood when she arrived, and then they kept her in hospital for two days.

2. The book .... by Ruth Rendell. It .... by Penguin Books in 1990, and next year it .... into French and German.

3. The toys .... in Taiwan. Then they .... to a number of European countries where they .... in large department stores.

4. The film .... in China and it .... by Bernardo Bertolucci. Next month it .... at the Cannes Film Festival.

5. St Paul's Cathedral .... by Sir Christopher Wren and it .... at the end of the 17th century. Both Nelson and Wellington .... there.

write	make (2)	design	take	publish	bury	give	export
show	build	translate	direct	sell			

2 Lexical sets

Arrange these words into three groups, and give each group a heading.

a general	ambulance	antibiotics	fight	doctor	prime minister
enemy	win	politician	cure	captain	lose	president
treat	shoot	emperor	war	accident	hospital

Complete the texts using *who, which, although* or *however*.

1. Monsieur de l'Orme, ... was the doctor to Louis XIII and XIV of France, believed that he would live longer if he stayed in warm places. When he was at home, he sat in a chair covered with blankets, and when he went out he wore a big coat, six pairs of stockings and several hats. He always had a piece of garlic in his mouth, incense in his ears and sticks of herb in his nose. He slept in an oven .... was surrounded by hot water bottles. .... he ate only sheep's tongues and fruit syrup, he lived until he was 94.

2. US President Rutherford Hayes, and his wife, ... was known as 'Lemonade Lucy', never drank alcohol, and they didn't allow any alcoholic drinks in the White House. ...., the butler was happy to provide guests with alcoholic drinks, ... he did for money. .... everybody else knew about it, the President himself never discovered his butler's little business.

4 From verb to noun   vocabulary: word building

Complete the table using a dictionary to help you.

Verb	Noun	Verb	Noun
die	*death*	elect	....
murder	....	explode	....
escape	....	develop	....
invade	....	assassinate	....
win	....	invent	....
resign	....	destroy	....

With two-syllable words or more, one syllable will have the main stress:

Examples: doctor   computer   understand   education

Now look at the verbs and nouns in Exercise 4. Where is the main stress on each of these words?

📼 Listen to the recording to check your answers, and practise saying the words.

6 The fate of the Russian royal family – fact or fiction?   reading

16th July, 1918: Tsar Nicolas II of Russia and his family were shot in Ekaterinburg (now Sverdlovsk) – or were they?

There are many different versions of the story of the Romanov family; some say that the Tsarina and her daughters in fact escaped. But one of the most famous accounts is that of Pavel Medvedev, who was an eye-witness to the event.

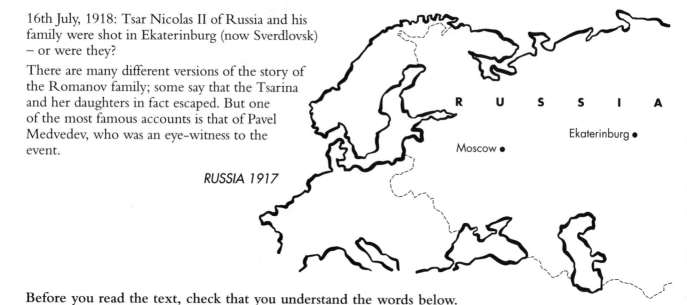

RUSSIA 1917

Before you read the text, check that you understand the words below.

heir: in this text, it is the eldest son who would become Tsar.
Tsar/ Tsarina: the Emperor/Empress of Russia.
to moan: to make a low, quiet noise if you are in pain.
wound (n) or (v): damage to the body caused by a knife or gun or other weapon; *gun* and *knife* are examples of *weapons*.

A Now read Pavel Medvedev's story of the murders.

In the evening of July 16th, Commandant Yurovsky (the head of the Guard) said to me, 'We must shoot them all tonight, so tell the guards not to be alarmed if they hear shots.' About midnight, Yurovsky woke up the Tsar's family. I do not know if they were told the reason ... and where they were to be taken. In about an hour, the whole of the family, the doctor, the maid and the waiters got up, washed and dressed themselves. Shortly after one o'clock they left their rooms. The Tsar carried the heir in his arms. During my presence none of the Tsar's family asked any questions. They did not weep or cry.

We entered a room on the ground floor of the house. Yurovsky's assistant brought three

chairs; one chair was for the Emperor, one for the Empress and the third for the heir. The Empress sat by the wall by the window. Behind her stood three of her daughters. The heir and the Emperor sat side by side almost in the middle of the room. Doctor Botkin stood behind the heir. The maid, a very tall woman, stood at the left of the door leading to the store room; by her side stood one of the Tsar's daughters (the fourth). Two servants stood against the wall on the left from the entrance of the room.

It seemed as if all of them guessed their fate, but not one of them made a single sound. At this moment, eleven men entered the room. Yurovsky ordered me to leave, saying, 'Go onto the street, see if anybody is there, and wait to see if the shots have been heard.'

I went out but before I got to the street, I heard the shots. I returned to the house immediately, where I saw that all members of the Tsar's family were on the floor with many wounds in their bodies. The doctor, the maid and the two waiters were also dead. The heir was still alive and moaned a little. Yurovsky went up and shot at him two or three more times. Then the heir was still.

B From the story, mark these sentences true or false.

1. The family didn't ask questions.
2. The chairs were brought by Yurovsky.
3. Eleven people were murdered that night.
4. Medvedev was not present at the actual shooting.
5. Yurovsky was told to leave the room where the Romanovs were to be shot.
6. The family were told that they were going to be shot.
7. Medvedev was sent into the street because Yurovsky did not want him to see the shooting.

7 Dictation

A ▭ Play the recording and write the sentences you hear in the spaces.

1. a. ....
   b. ....
   ....

2. a. ....
   b. ....
   ....

3. a. ....
   b. ....
   ....

4. a. ....
   b. ....
   ....

B Now rewrite each pair of sentences to make one sentence using *who* or *which*.

Example: a. *The bus arrived late.*
         b. *It was full of noisy children.*
         The bus which arrived late was full of noisy children.

8 Speaking partners

Think about the following questions and discuss them with your speaking partner.

1. In your opinion what are the three most important events in world history in the twentieth century?
2. In your opinion what are the three most important events in your country's history in the twentieth century?
3. Do you ever read about history now, or watch TV programmes about it? If so, tell your speaking partner.
4. What do you know about the history of your family?
5. What can you tell your partner about the history of the place where you live?
6. What do you know about the history of the place where you have your English lessons?
7. What do you think of the account in Exercise 6? Do you think it is true or not?

9 Reflections

This space is for you to make a note of things you have learnt in this unit. You can also use it as a diary to write about your problems and progress in English.

23

WHOSE LIFE IS IT ANYWAY?

A Look at the table below.

I call him by his first name.
I call her by her family name/surname.
I call them by their title.

I call him Jimmy.
I call her Miss Leech.
I call them Mr and Mrs Raman.
I call him/her Doctor.
I call him Sir.
I call her Madam.
I call her Mum.

I don't call him anything.
I don't call them anything.

How do you address these people when you are speaking to them? Write sentences using the language in the table above.

	Joumana	Stefan
1. your friends		
2. your doctor		
3. your teacher		
4. your boss		
5. your landlord or landlady		
6. your dentist		
7. a stranger in the street		
8. your tax inspector		
9. a waiter in a restaurant		
10. your grandparents		
11. your newspaper seller		
12. your bank manager		
13. your parents		

B ☐☐ Now listen to the recording. You will hear two people talking about how they address these people. Write their answers in the table.

C What about writing? If you write a letter to the people below, how do you begin?

Example: *your doctor*
I write 'Dear Doctor Cobbe'

1. your doctor
2. your English teacher
3. your tax inspector
4. a lawyer you have never met
5. your boss

Complete the sentences using an adjective or adverb from the list.

careful	patiently	dangerously	efficient	beautifully	peacefully
fast	hard	slowly	nervous	peaceful	easily	terrible	quietly

1. It's raining .... at the moment.

2. She died .... in bed at the age of 88.

3. I spent a .... afternoon, sitting in a field reading a book.

4. I waited .... for half an hour and then I began to get angry.

5. I was very .... while the teacher read out the exam results.

6. I could sing .... when I was a child, but now I have a .... voice.

7. If you speak too ...., people won't be able to hear you.

8. You can be arrested for driving ....

9. I always drive .... in bad weather.

10. It was a .... race, but she still won ....

11. He's always very .... with his money.

12. I've got a very .... secretary who does things before I ask for them.

A Look at this example:

Is it to do with finance?
 Yes, it's a financial problem. ....

When we say that one thing is *to do with* another thing, we mean it is connected in some way.

Now respond to these questions in a similar way, changing the noun to an adjective in your reply.

1. Is it to do with religion?

   Yes, it's a ....

2. Is it to do with education?

   Yes, ...

3. Is it to do with politics?

   ....

4. Is it to do with culture?

   ....

5. Is it to do with society?

   ....

B This time you must change verbs into nouns. Complete these sentences using nouns formed from the verb.

Example: *You must decide.*
         You must make *a decision.* ....

6. You must choose. You must make ....

7. Can we compare them? Can we make ....?

8. Are they getting divorced? Are they getting ....?

9. Can you advise me? Can you give me ....?

10. What do you believe in? What are ....?

4 Sounds and spelling

Look at the sounds circled in the words in Box A below. Find the same sounds in the words in Box B and underline them. Draw lines between the words with the same sounds.

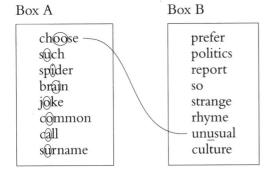

Box A

choose
such
spider
brain
joke
common
call
surname

Box B

prefer
politics
report
so
strange
rhyme
unusual
culture

▭▭ Listen to the recording to correct your answers. Then practise saying the pairs of words together.

Example: *choose – unusual*

5 The origins of first names

In the English speaking world, first names come from many different sources. Some are from the Bible (for example, Rachel, Matthew), while others are Celtic or Anglo Saxon (such as Alfred). The Puritans introduced the use of abstract nouns as names (for instance, Faith and Prudence). In the 19th century, it was fashionable to use the names of jewels, flowers and months of spring (Pearl, Rosemary and April). In the 20th century, TV and cinema have influenced the choice of first names (Cary, Marilyn, Meryl).

Do names have similar origins in your language?

Look at the names in the box below. Do you have similar names to these in your language? If so, think of someone you know, and check the origin of the name in the text below.

| Mary | Elizabeth | John | Charles |

Mary
From a name in the Bible in a variety of forms; possibly Hebrew meaning *rebellion* or *wished-for child*, also in the New Testament in the form of the Virgin Mary, Mary Magdalene. For several hundred years, people thought it was too sacred to have as a first name.
Variants: Maria, Marian, Marie, Marietta, Marilyn, Marion, Marisa, Maura, Maureen, Moira

Elizabeth
From the Hebrew name, Elisheba meaning *oath of God* or *God is satisfaction*. An Old Testament name, which became popular in the time of Queen Elizabeth the First in the 16th century, and is still commonly used today.
Variants: Babette, Bettina, Elise, Elissa, Elsa, Elspeth, Ilsa, Isabel, Isabella, Isabelle, Isobel, Liesel, Liesl, Lise, Lisette

John

From the Hebrew, meaning *Jehovah is gracious*, the Latin name being Johannes. Very popular in the Christian world, because of St John the Baptist as well as St John, one of the four apostles from the New Testament. By the end of the 16th century, John was one of the most common names in the English speaking world.

Variants: Hans, Iain, Jan, Ivan, Juan, Sean
Feminine forms: Jane, Janet, Jean, Jeanne, Joan, Joanna, Joanne

Charles

From old English and old German words meaning *man*. The French form of the name was made popular in the 9th century by Charles the Great (Charlemagne) and used by many other European kings.

Variants: Carl, Carlo, Carlos, Carol, Karl
Feminine forms: Carlotta, Carol, Carola, Charlotte, Charlene, Caroline

Read through all the explanations above. Then do the exercise below.

Memory test. See how many questions you can answer without looking at the texts.

1. Does Charles mean *man* or *rebellion*?
2. What is Marilyn a variant of?
3. Does Elizabeth come from Hebrew or Greek?
4. Is Johannes a Hebrew or a Latin name?
5. Do Ivan and Ilsa have the same origin?
6. Which name was popular with European kings?

Check your answers by looking at the texts again.

---

6 Expressing preferences

⟂ Listen to the recording. The teacher will suggest doing something. Tell him you agree, or tell him what you would prefer to do / rather do. Choose from the examples:

Example: TEACHER: *Shall we practise listening?*
　　　　　YOU:　　*Yes, all right.*
　　　　　or　　　*I'd rather practise speaking.*
　　　　　or　　　*I'd prefer to practise writing.*

Choices:
1. listening / reading / speaking / writing
2. go to the laboratory / carry on working / have a break
3. do a test / play a game / sing a song
4. do some pronunciation practice / study some grammar / study some vocabulary
5. revise some expressions / watch a video / do a dictation
6. practise the present perfect / practise asking questions / practise prepositions
7. work in groups / work in pairs / work alone

---

7 Good morning

You are going to write a paragraph about the sequence of events when you woke up this morning. Look at this example:

It was a very sunny morning and I was woken up by the sound of birds outside my window. I got up – before the alarm went off – and had a cold shower. I felt really good after that, and I went to the kitchen and made some fresh coffee. I wanted to have some toast, but we didn't have any bread, so on my way to work I bought some fruit and a sandwich. I had to wait twenty minutes for a bus, but I didn't mind because it was such a nice day. I still got to work on time, and I read the paper for ten minutes before starting work.

What happened to you this morning? Write it here.

....

....

....

....

....

....

....

8 Speaking partners

Tell your partner the names of the members of your family, and ask each other questions about them.

- How did they get their names?
- Do you know the meaning of their names?
- Do they like their names?
- Do you have any nicknames, or special names in the family?
- What does your surname mean?

9 Reflections

This space is for you to make a note of things you have learnt in this unit. You can also use it as a diary to write about your problems and progress in English.

....

....

....

....

....

....

....

....

....

....

....

....

....

CINEMA AND THE ARTS

1 Test your knowledge

Find a connection between the names in the first column and the names in the third column. Then use the verbs in the second column to make sentences in the past simple active or passive.

Examples: *Al Pacino starred in* The Godfather.
Citizen Kane *was directed by Orson Welles.*

Al Pacino	play	Richard Burton
Citizen Kane	write	Richard Rogers
Shakespeare	compose	*Eleanor Rigby*
Duke Ellington	conduct	*The Godfather*
War and Peace	direct	Pablo Picasso
Gabriel García Márquez	design	*The Seven Samurai*
The Marriage of Figaro	paint	Tolstoy
The Pompidou Centre	star	piano
Guernica	marry	Hitchcock
Elizabeth Taylor	sing	Orson Welles
Psycho		*100 Years of Solitude*
The Beatles		the Berlin Philharmonic Orchestra
Akira Kurosawa		*Macbeth*
Herbert von Karajan		Mozart

2 Theatre and cinema

Complete the network using the following words:

poet   costume designer   holographer   director   composer   musician
fashion designer   artist   opera singer   conductor   dramatist
actor/actress   photographer   sculptor   architect   novelist

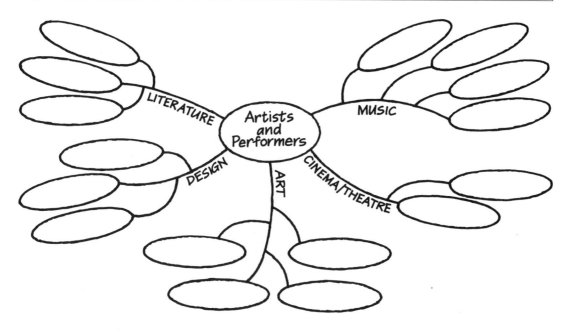

3 Crossword

Complete the following crossword.

Across

1. Someone who tells the truth is this. (6)
5. Past tense of *meet*. (3)
7. A play or film will have one of these in the newspaper. Sometimes it's good and sometimes it's bad. (6)
9. Margot Fonteyn is a famous example. (9)
10. One way of paying for theatre tickets. (4)
11. You may have one of these in your eye after a very sad film. (4)
14. Famous Spanish painter. (4)
15 and 21. Foreign films often have these. (3, 6)
17. Musical instrument, often played in church. (5)
19. Children's stories often begin with this word. (4)

Down

1. You can buy books in paperback or .... (8)
2. Gabriel García Márquez is one. (8)
3. Spielberg's first name. (6)
4. Famous line from *Hamlet*: To ...... or not to .... (2)
6. The place where you see a play. (7)
8. In America it's called the movies. (6)
12. When you sing or play an instrument on your own. (4)
13. A film or play that makes you laugh is this. (5)
16. Famous ballet by Tchaikovsky: *Swan* .... (4)
18. Famous line spoken by James Cagney: You dirty .... (3)
20. Famous science fiction film. (2)

4 First names in English

Divide the names into the categories in the table, according to the sound underlined. Listen to check your answers, then practise saying them.

Sheila	Andrew	Paul	Lorna	Joan	Stephen	Jean	Stewart
Rose	Leo	George	Julia	Laura	Neil	Judy	

Names that have the sound /iː/

....

Names that have the sound /uː/

....

Names that have the sound /ɔː/

....

Names that have the sound /əʊ/

....

Which are men's names and which are women's? Can you think of any famous people with these names?

Read the texts and match them with the pictures.

A Woody Allen, film director, writer and actor   B Carlo Maria Giulini, conductor

C Mitsuko Uchida, pianist

D Stephen King, horror novelist

1. X, now in his seventies, is recognised as one of the greatest X in the world, but he waited more than twenty years before leading the works of Mozart, Bach and Beethoven. Why? Because he did not feel ready. 'I have to understand a score, believe in it and love every note,' says X. 'If those three conditions are not fulfilled, then I cannot conduct the work.'

2. 'It happens this way. I'm sitting at home and I get this great idea. Then I cast it and find the locations and they're not quite so wonderful. By the time I shoot it, I think, "This isn't what I wanted to do." But it's too late to change. And by the time it comes out, it's so far off the mark that I'm sick of it.'

3. X says that people often ask what scares him. 'Everything,' is his answer. 'Aeroplanes. Elevators. The dark is a big one. I always switch the light on when I leave a hotel room because I think about coming back to a strange room, feeling for the light and having a hand close over mine. One of the reasons why I do the job I do is because it's a kind of psychological protection. My mother used to say, "If you think the worst, it can't come true."'

4. 'In my work, I believe one's life should depend on what one is convinced about and driven to do. The rest is irrelevant. And when the world likes what you are doing, you just say, "Thank you, aren't I lucky?" If not, you just keep doing it. You must always believe that tomorrow you will play better. The doubts keep you alive.'

6 Playing in a band

A 📼 Listen to Spencer talking about the band he plays in, and complete the following sentences.

1. The band is called ....

2. Altogether there are .... people in the band.

3. The band was formed ....

4. Spencer plays ....

5. They mostly play .... music.

6. They perform in .... and ....

7. They usually practise .... times a month.

8. .... writes most of the music they play.

B Write questions for the above answers.

Example: 1. *What's the band called?*
        or
        What's the name of the band?

7 Film diary

If you often go to the cinema, you could keep a diary in English of the films that you see. Something like this:

TITLE	*Tootsie*
TYPE OF FILM	Comedy
DIRECTED BY	Sydney Pollack
STARRED	Dustin Hoffman and Jessica Lange
SUMMARY	An actor, played by Dustin Hoffman, dresses up as a woman in order to get a part in a TV programme. He falls in love with the leading lady, who thinks he is a woman. This creates problems for Hoffman, but is also the reason for much of the comedy.

8 Speaking partners

If your speaking partner also goes to the cinema a lot, you could test each other in English, like this:

Examples: *What type of film is* A Fish called Wanda?
          Who directed Psycho?
          Who starred in Midnight Cowboy?
          What is The Last Emperor *about?*

Tell each other about the last film you saw.

9 Visual dictionary

Complete the visual dictionary on page 131 using a bilingual dictionary to help you.

This space is for you to make a note of things you have learnt in this unit. You can also use it as a diary to write about your problems and progress in English.

....

....

....

....

....

....

....

....

....

....

....

....

....

VISUAL DICTIONARY

1. ....
2. ....
3. ....
4. ....
5. ....
6. ....
7. ....
8. ....
9. ....
10. ....
11. ....
12. ....
13. ....
14. ....
15. ....
16. ....
17. ....
18. ....
19. ....

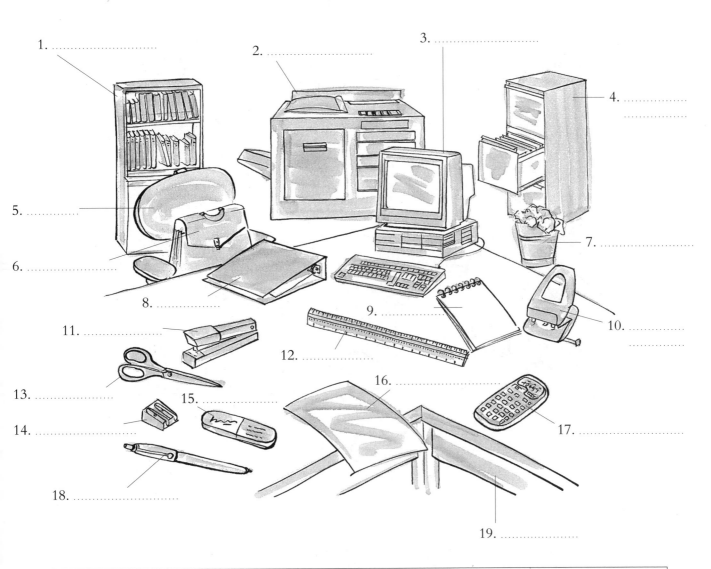

desk	chair	wastepaper bin	photocopier	filing cabinet	bookcase	rubber
pencil sharpener	ruler	ballpoint pen	file	word processor	notebook	
hole punch	stapler	scissors	briefcase	calculator	sheet of paper	

MORE NEW WORDS

....
....
....
....
....
....

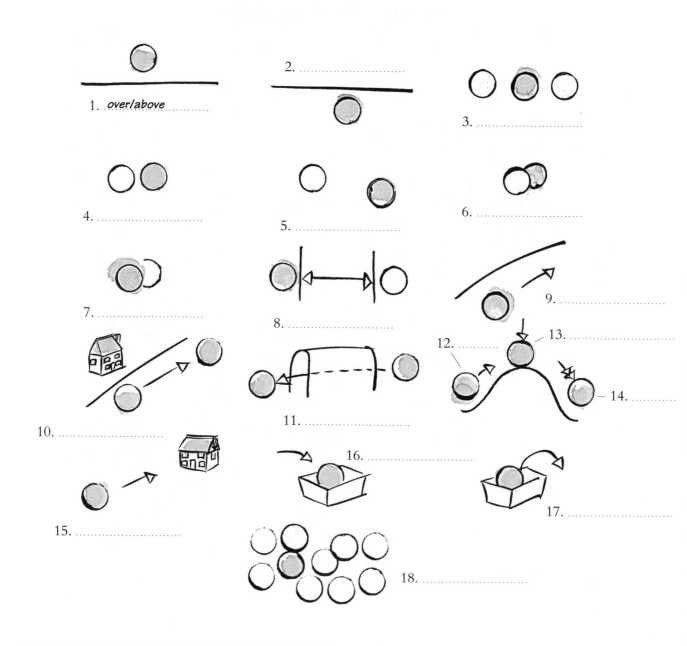

1. *over/above*
2. ....
3. ....
4. ....
5. ....
6. ....
7. ....
8. ....
9. ....
10. ....
11. ....
12. ....
13. ....
14. ....
15. ....
16. ....
17. ....
18. ....

between	out of	up	near	on / on top (of)	in front of	along	over/above
next to	past	opposite	through	down	behind	towards	into	among
under/below							

MORE NEW WORDS

....
....
....
....
....
....

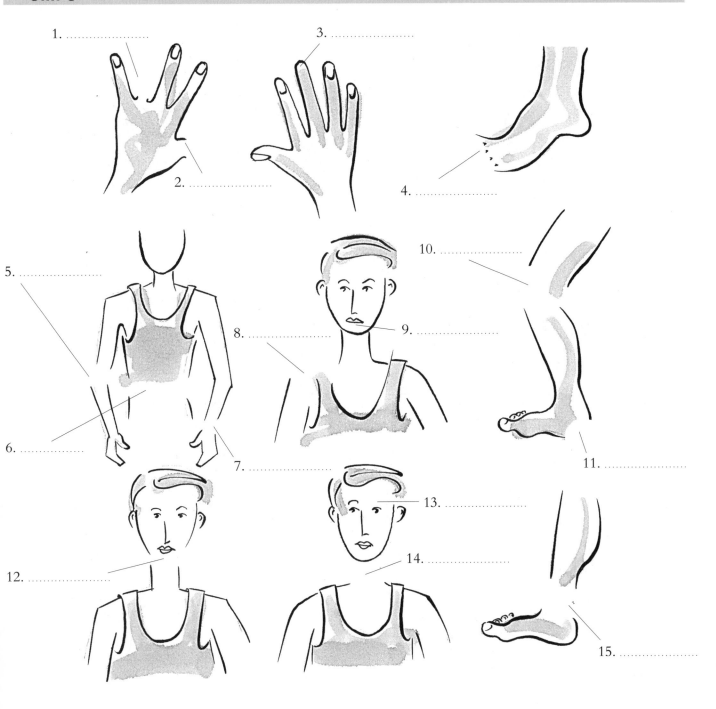

1. ....

2. ....

3. ....

4. ....

5. ....

6. ....

7. ....

8. ....

9. ....

10. ....

11. ....

12. ....

13. ....

14. ....

15. ....

| waist | eyebrow | chin | knee | ankle | nail | elbow | finger | neck | heel |
| thumb | shoulder | lip | wrist | toes |

MORE NEW WORDS

....

....

....

....

....

....

1. ....
2. ....
3. ....
4. ....
5. ....
6. ....
7. ....
8. ....
9. ....
10. ....
11. ....
12. ....
13. ....
14. ....
15. ....
16. ....
17. ....
18. ....
19. ....

| suit | sweater/jumper | gloves | tie | skirt | belt | trousers | scarf | blouse |
| raincoat | jacket | shirt | | | | | | |

| put on | try on | turn off | turn down | take off | turn up | turn on |

MORE NEW WORDS

....
....
....
....
....
....

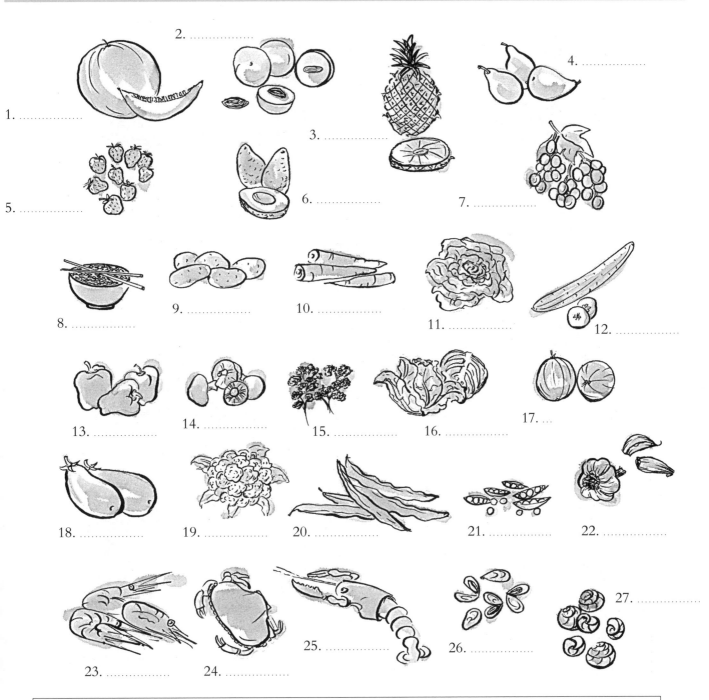

1. ....
2. ....
3. ....
4. ....
5. ....
6. ....
7. ....
8. ....
9. ....
10. ....
11. ....
12. ....
13. ....
14. ....
15. ....
16. ....
17. ...
18. ....
19. ....
20. ....
21. ....
22. ....
23. ....
24. ....
25. ....
26. ....
27. ....

cauliflower	grapes	mushrooms	crab	cabbage	pears	strawberries	peppers
aubergines	snails	avocado	prawns	rice	potatoes	mussels	carrots
lettuce	melon	garlic	parsley	peaches	onions	beans	peas	lobster
pineapple	cucumber						

MORE NEW WORDS

....
....
....
....
....
....

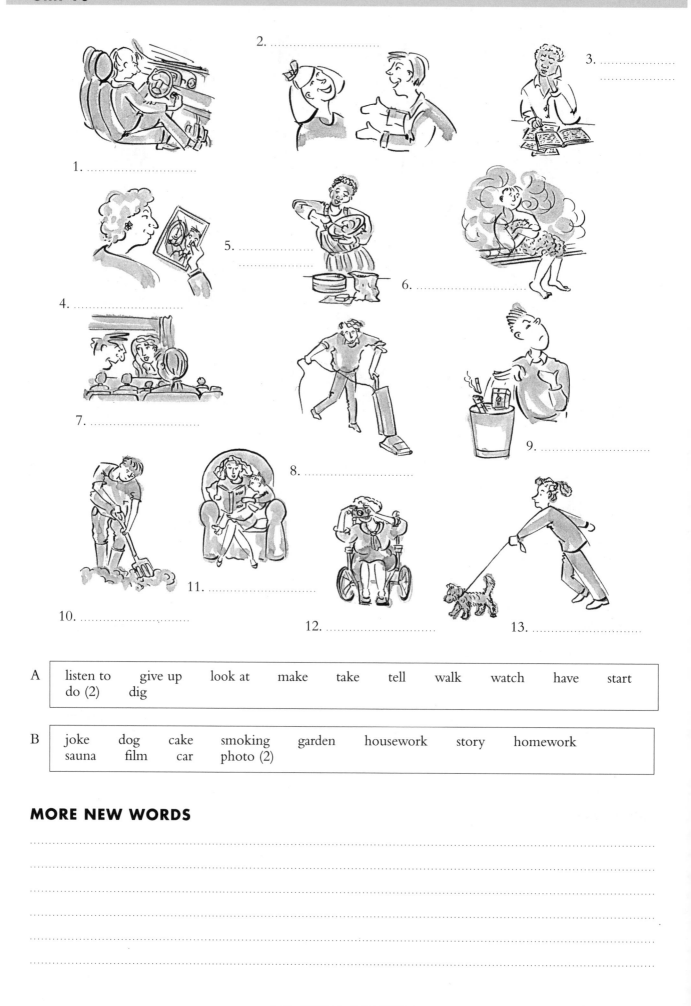

1. ....
2. ....
3. ....
   ....
4. ....
5. ....
   ....
6. ....
7. ....
8. ....
9. ....
10. ....
11. ....
12. ....
13. ....

A	listen to	give up	look at	make	take	tell	walk	watch	have	start
	do (2)	dig								

B	joke	dog	cake	smoking	garden	housework	story	homework
	sauna	film	car	photo (2)				

MORE NEW WORDS

....
....
....
....
....
....

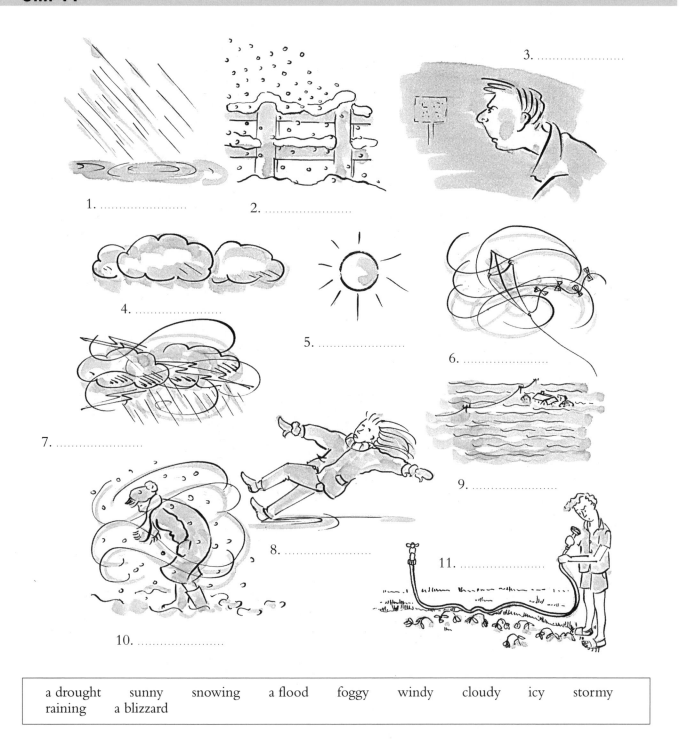

1. ....

2. ....

3. ....

4. ....

5. ....

6. ....

7. ....

8. ....

9. ....

10. ....

11. ....

a drought	sunny	snowing	a flood	foggy	windy	cloudy	icy	stormy
raining	a blizzard							

MORE NEW WORDS

....

....

....

....

....

....

1. ....
2. ....
3. ....
4. ....
5. ....
6. ....
7. ....
8. ....
9. ....
10. ....
11. ....
12. ....
13. ....

duty-free shop	check-in	scales	luggage	queue	passport control
security check	customs officer	left luggage lockers	departure lounge	bar
aircraft taking off	aircraft landing			

MORE NEW WORDS

....
....
....
....
....
....

1. ....
2. ....
3. ....
4. ....
5. ....
6. ....
7. ....
8. ....
9. ....
10. ....
11. ....
12. ....
13. ....
14. ....
15. ....
16. ....
17. ....
18. ....
19. ....
20. ....
21. ....
22. ....
23. ....
24. ....
25. ....
26. ....
27. ....
28. ....

wardrobe	toilet	mobile phone	path	roof	chest of drawers	study
chimney	washbasin	bookcase	bath	french windows	shower	lounge
armchair	double bed	coffee table	portrait	bedroom	desk	hi-fi	hall
bedside table	computer	rug	fireplace	calculator	bathroom

MORE NEW WORDS

....
....
....
....
....
....

1. ....
2. ....
3. ....
4. ....
5. ....
6. ....
7. ....
8. ....
9. ....
10. ....
11. ....
12. ....
13. ....
14. ....
15. ....
16. ....

sheep	rocks	yacht	lorry	pedestrian crossing	clouds	pedestrians
motor cycle	postbox	field	fence	beach	tractor	traffic lights	gate	sea

MORE NEW WORDS

....
....
....
....
....
....

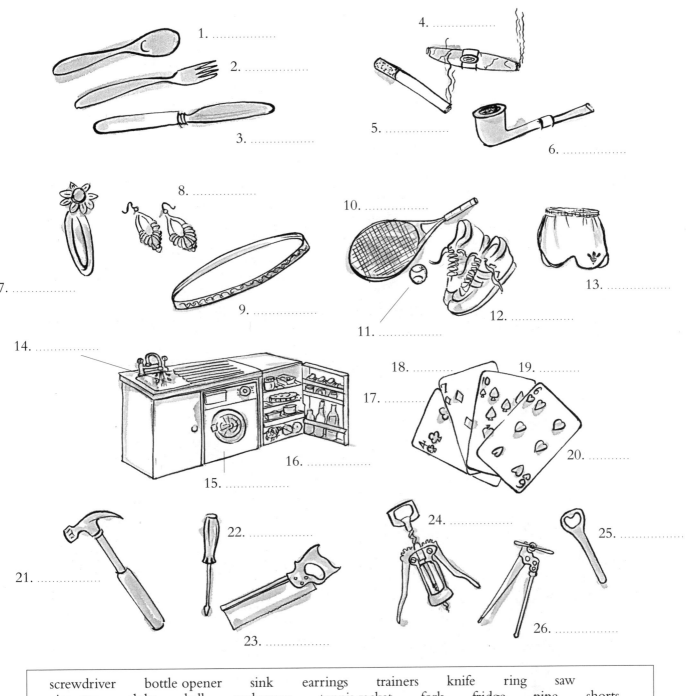

1. ....
2. ....
3. ....
4. ....
5. ....
6. ....
7. ....
8. ....
9. ....
10. ....
11. ....
12. ....
13. ....
14. ....
15. ....
16. ....
17. ....
18. ....
19. ....
20. ....
21. ....
22. ....
23. ....
24. ....
25. ....
26. ....

screwdriver	bottle opener	sink	earrings	trainers	knife	ring	saw
cigarette	clubs	ball	corkscrew	tennis racket	fork	fridge	pipe	shorts
hearts	spoon	cigar	spades	washing machine	hammer	diamonds	bracelet
tin/can opener							

MORE NEW WORDS

....

....

....

....

....

....

MORE NEW WORDS

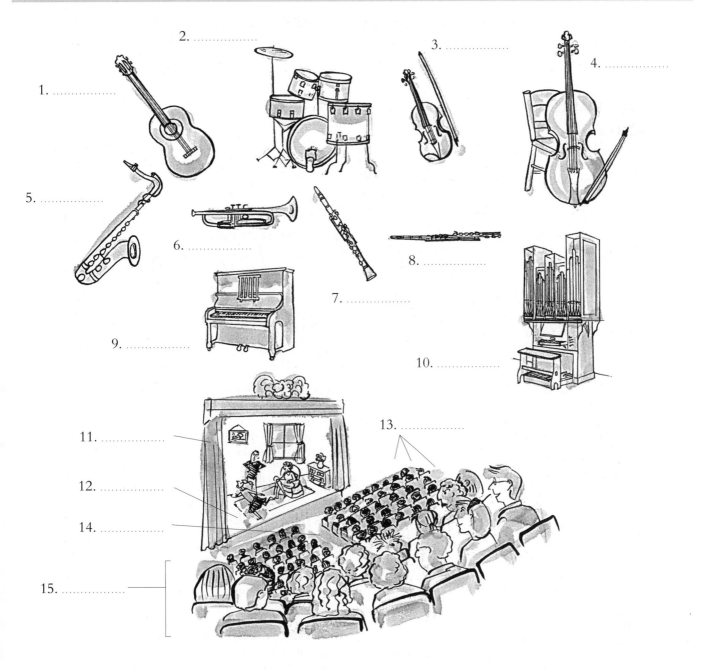

1. ....
2. ....
3. ....
4. ....
5. ....
6. ....
7. ....
8. ....
9. ....
10. ....
11. ....
12. ....
13. ....
14. ....
15. ....

| clarinet | cello | drums | flute | violin | guitar | saxophone | trumpet | piano |
| organ | | | | | | | | |

| curtain | audience | aisle | stage | rows |

MORE NEW WORDS

....
....
....
....
....
....

TAPESCRIPTS

1 GETTING STARTED

6 Correct the text

There are a lot of mistakes in this text. You need a pencil to correct them in your book.

Now, in the first line, the word *fortune-teller* should have a hyphen in the middle. Put one in.

There should also be a full stop after the word *once*.

Mr Chatterjee's name on the first line is spelt incorrectly. It should be double *t* in the middle.

Near the end of this sentence, there are brackets round the phrase *in the middle of the bazaar*. These brackets are unnecessary, so cross them out.

In the next sentence, you will notice that part of Mr Chatterjee's name is missing. Could you just complete it, please.

Tarot should have a capital *T*, and at the end of the paragraph, you need a question mark after *why not*.

In the next line, you can leave out the word *also*, but you do need a comma after the word *too*.

Finally, in the last sentence, you need an apostrophe before the *t* in the word *don't*.

2 ASKING QUESTIONS

4 Catch the pronoun *and*
5 Stress and rhythm

1. When did you first meet him?
2. Where did you meet her?
3. How often do you see them?
4. How far is it to her house?
5. Why do you like her?
6. When did you last see him?
7. How often do you phone them?
8. Why did you leave him?

6 Kangaroos

A: So – why do kangaroos hop?
B: Well, no one really knows. Um, maybe because they carry babies in their pouches, so it's easier and it's safer for them to be upright, especially if they have to travel really fast across rocky ground.
A: Do they have any enemies?
B: Oh, yes, yes, they do. Quite a lot of animals attack them – um large birds of prey, large lizards, pythons, dingoes, er, and of course human beings, who kill them for their meat.
A: It's a funny name, kangaroo. Where did that come from?
B: Well, there's a story – but it's a ... I'm not sure if true or not – that Captain Cook, the explorer, er, when he went to Australia, he asked the Aborigines what the name of this very strange animal was. And the Aborigines said *kangaroo* which means *I don't know* in their language – so Cook mistakenly called them *kangaroos*.
A: Are they friendly to humans?
B: Yes, they are quite friendly in some areas, but they are generally very timid. Um, they do defend themselves against other animals like dogs, though. And if you keep kangaroos in a zoo, when you go down to the cage, you have to bend down, because if you stand upright, they see it as an aggressive posture.

A: Do they live in groups?
B: Oh, yes, yes, they certainly do. They live and travel together in very large groups of up to about 100. And there is always a leader – obviously the strongest and largest male, and he keeps the younger kangaroos in control by kicking and boxing.

3 STREETLIFE

3 Picture dictation

Down the middle of your map, from top to bottom, there is a river. And across the middle of your map, from left to right, there is a main road with a bridge going over the river.

Now, to the right of the river, just above the bridge, there is a cathedral. Draw it on your map.

In the top left-hand corner of your map there is a castle. Put it on the map.

There is another road, called Devon Road, which begins just below the castle, goes over the river, round the back of the cathedral, and then joins the main road.

Devon Road continues the other side of the main road, goes into a roundabout and disappears off the bottom of your map.

To the right of Devon Road, between the main road and the roundabout there is a supermarket.

Now go back from the roundabout to the main road, turn left, go over the bridge, and there is a road on your left. This road runs almost parallel with the river and disappears off the bottom of the map. Next to the road, near the bottom of the map, there is a factory. The factory is not on the same side as the river, but the opposite side of the road.

Now go back up the road to the main road, turn left, and there is another road on your right. This road goes to the castle. Also on this road, midway between the castle and the main road, is the railway station. It is on the Devon Road side.

Right, there's your map, which you will now need to do the next exercise.

6 A bad sense of direction

1. Gareth

I got very lost recently with some colleagues in a car, er, in San Antonio in Texas, and I was driving, but of course in America they drive on a different side of the road, and I kept missing a turn-off and going round in circles on this very wide, very long road and it took us an hour and a half to find our way back home.

2. Lynn

Well I got lost in a wood in the middle of Dartmoor, er, and I was with my whole family including some small children, and in fact my family live in Devon so we went out and didn't take a map with us, so once we realised that we'd got to a place where we didn't know exactly where we were, of course we couldn't look at a map to tell us. And one of us just said, 'Oh, yes, I know where we're going' and we blindly followed him and of course got to the end of the path and didn't know where we were. Anyway we kept on walking for about an hour I think, and finally came to a road where we could ask some directions.

3. Ian

I got lost this New Year's Eve at about 11 o'clock at night. We, a group of us, climb a hill every New Year's Eve near where I live. And we climb to the top, and aim to get there by midnight, have a drink, and come back down again. The hill is about 800 feet. And we went up the hill in clear moonlight and perfect weather and got to the top and had a drink, and then the mist descended on us. And we began to find our way down and we couldn't find our way down off this hill, and wandered around in circles for about two hours with people swearing at us and telling us we should have taken lights, etc. and finally a group of drunken revellers rescued us.

4 CREATIVITY

2 Dictation

1. A: Have you ever made a speech?
   B: Yes, I made one last week at a wedding.
2. A: I've met lots of famous people.
   B: Really? Who?
   A: Well, I met the Italian football team a couple of years ago.
3. A: Have you heard about Jean?
   B: Heard what?
   A: She's left her husband.
   B: Yes, I know. She left him at the weekend.
4. A: I can't come tonight.
   B: Why?
   A: I've spent all my money.
   B: Oh!
   A: Yes, I bought a hi-fi yesterday.

5 Weak vowels and word stress

angry: She was angry with her brother.
confused: I was very confused after the accident.
embarrassed: He was embarrassed when he saw her.
umbrella: I forgot my umbrella yesterday.
Japan: Have you ever been to Japan?
connect: You must connect both ends.
apologise: Don't apologise for being late.
collar: What size collar are you?
panic: Try not to panic.
comma: You need a comma in this sentence.

7 Creative visualisation

Have you ever been for a walk in your head? Shut your eyes and take this tour.

You are walking in a forest. It's a beautiful, sunny day, and the plants and trees are tall and green.

Can you see them? Imagine the colours.

You keep walking into the forest. There are more trees, so it's getting darker now, but you feel comfortable.

What can you smell?

Can you feel the plants? How do they feel?

Suddenly you come to a building in the forest. It's a small house. Imagine the house and the garden around it. How many windows are there? Is it modern or old? Look into one of the windows. What do you see?

Go to the front door and open it. Someone is waiting for you inside. Who is it? Why are they there? How do you feel now? Follow the dream to the end. When you have finished, write about your walk and what happened.

If you like, give it to your teacher to look at, or show it to your speaking partner. If you prefer, don't show it to anyone.

5 YOU AND YOUR BODY

7 Body factfile

Are you male or female?
How old are you?
How tall are you?
How much do you weigh?
What colour is your hair?
What about your eyes?
What size shoes do you take?
Do you wear glasses or contact lenses?
How often do you take pills for aches and pains?
Do you eat meals at regular times?
How much sleep do you get every night?
When did you last have a dental check-up?
Is there an illness you often get? If so, what?
What do you do to keep in good physical condition?
How do you feel right now?

6 LEARNING – PAST AND PRESENT

7 What can you do?

1. Can you practise your pronunciation and laugh at the same time?
2. Can you put your hand up and get up at the same time?
3. Can you study effectively and talk on the phone at the same time?
4. Can you find out the meaning of a new word and learn how to pronounce it at the same time?
5. Can you work under stress and feel relaxed at the same time?
6. Can you teach someone how to do something and learn how to do something yourself at the same time?
7. Can you apologise for something and ask for something at the same time?
8. Can you look after children and do your job effectively at the same time?
9. Can you use a computer and speak a foreign language at the same time?
10. Can you do this exercise and listen to the radio at the same time?

7 LETTERS THAT TELL A STORY

2 A leopard is faster than a camel

1. A leopard is faster than a camel.
2. Hepatitis is more serious than a sore throat.
3. A lake is bigger than a pond.
4. A week is shorter than a fortnight.
5. A gun is more dangerous than a knife.
6. Oranges are sweeter than lemons.
7. A three-star hotel is more expensive than a guest house.
8. An adult is older than a teenager.
9. A word processor is more useful than a typewriter.
10. A caravan is more comfortable than a tent.
11. A motorway is wider than a street.
12. A dentist is better-paid than a dustman.

6 Learning to write

Lynn

I was four when I started to learn to write. My grandfather started to teach me before I went to school. I do remember that I always found the capital letters much easier to write than the small letters. And I remember that once we started writing in school we weren't allowed to use pens, we had to use pencils until we became really good at writing. I can write a few characters in Chinese now, but not very many. As far as my normal writing is concerned, er, I have two styles of handwriting: one for other people and one for myself, and most people think that when I'm really trying hard, my writing is easy to read and looks quite good, uh, and I think it looks quite impressive too.

Gareth

I started to learn to write when I first went to school at the age of five. And I remember having to write neatly between two lines on a piece of paper, and we wrote with wooden pens and ink, and you had to be very careful that you didn't leave blots on the paper. The only other script I can write apart from my English joined-up writing is a little Old Testament Greek because I had to study it once. But I've forgotten how to do that, so the only writing I can do now is in my rather large sprawling hand which looks fine at a distance but people tell me when they try to read it, it's almost illegible – but I think it looks rather good.

8 TAKE IT OR LEAVE IT

4 Sounds similar

1. I'll leave him now and don't try and stop me!
2. I can afford it at the moment.
3. Are you going to try and get your money back?
4. My sister's lent me the money.
5. We'll have to take it back tomorrow.
6. I paid for it in cash.
7. I've seen her today.
8. I work for nothing.

6 Listen and answer

These questions are about shops:
Is there a greengrocer's near your home?
Where do you buy your daily paper?
Do you ever buy things in a department store?
What was the last thing you bought in a clothes shop?
And now some questions about paying for things:
Do you pay for anything by direct debit?
Do you often lend people money?
Do most shops accept credit cards in your country?
How do you pay for your English classes?
And finally some questions about shopping:
Do you always try clothes on before you buy them?
Do all clothes shops in your country have changing rooms?
Do you ever take things back to shops?
What do you do with the receipts for things you have bought?

9 FOOD AND DRINK

6 What's on the menu?

1.
A: What's the soup of the day?
B: It's cabbage and onion.
A: Fine, I'll have that.

2.
A: What's Chicken à la Basque, exactly?
B: Well, it's a kind of casserole; the chicken is cooked in wine and tomatoes, with garlic, onion and peppers.
A: That sounds nice – I'll have that.

3.
A: What's in the Salad Provençale?
B: Well, it's a bit like Salad Niçoise. It's got lettuce, tomatoes and cucumber, egg, olives ...
A: Egg?
B: Yeah, hard boiled egg, olives and french beans.
A: OK, I'll have that. It sounds interesting.

4.
A: What flavour ice cream have you got?
B: Um, there's strawberry, vanilla, peach, pineapple and chocolate.
A: Oh, could I have a mixture of strawberry and chocolate, please?
B: Yes, of course.

5.
A: What's Pizza della Casa, exactly?
B: It's a pizza topped with salami, peppers and mushrooms.
A: Fine. I'll have that.
B: Very good, sir.

10 FEELINGS: THE GOOD, THE BAD AND THE UGLY

4 Sounds missing.

Examples
He's the best teacher.
She wore a dark coat.
1. Is it your first time?
2. There are some magazines on the table.
3. She's a very old dog.
4. Her voice sounded strange.
5. I took a black cab to the station.
6. She bought some cheap perfume.
7. He told us a nice story.
8. We've got a small light in the garden.

6 Do you like blue?

1. Physical exercise makes me feel quite happy and fit.
2. I really like chocolate. It makes me feel warm inside.
3. I really like cool beer because it refreshes you, particularly if you've been doing exercise.
4. Rock music makes me feel old.
5. I really like good wine. I think it makes me very sociable.
6. The colour green makes me feel rested and relaxed.
7. The thought of raw egg makes me feel quite sick.
8. I can't stand hot weather. It makes me very bad-tempered.
9. Travelling on public transport makes me so angry I could scream sometimes.
10. The colour blue makes me feel calm and relaxed.
11. Birthdays make me feel like I'm a child again.

11 WEATHER

6 Seasonal Affective Disorder

In winter many people spend a lot of time indoors, and for many of us we get up in the dark, and by the time we leave work or school it's dark again. A surprising number of people are affected by these conditions and there is even a name for this winter depression – Seasonal Affective Disorder or SAD.

The most important symptom is depression, closely followed by the desire to sleep all the time. Some people also suffer from anxiety, some eat more, and others are more sensitive to pain, such as headaches and pains in their arms and legs. What actually causes SAD? Experts think that it is caused by a hormonal problem – some people produce too much of this hormone at night, especially in the winter, when the sunlight can't regulate it.

There is also evidence that this is only a problem in parts of the world which have a cold, dark winter – there is very little evidence of it near the equator.

Some patients are treated by photo-therapy: they sit under special lights for a few hours every day; and some feel immediate improvement after the first treatment.

12 ROMANCE

4 What happened and when?

1a. I fell off my bike while I was riding to school, but fortunately I didn't hurt myself.
1b. I fell off my bike while I was riding to school and unfortunately I broke my ankle.
2a. My legs got burnt when I was sunbathing, but fortunately I had some cream to put on them.
2b. My legs got burnt when I was sunbathing and unfortunately I didn't have anything to stop the pain.
3a. I dropped a plate while I was drying the dishes, but fortunately it was a cheap one.
3b. I dropped a plate while I was drying the dishes and unfortunately it broke.
4a. The zip broke when I was getting dressed, but fortunately I had another pair of trousers.
4b. The zip broke when I was getting dressed and unfortunately I couldn't mend it.
5a. I made a mistake while I was adding up the figures, but fortunately it didn't matter.
5b. I made a mistake while I was adding up the figures and unfortunately it was very important.
6a. The filling came out when I was cleaning my teeth, but fortunately I had a dental appointment the same day.
6b. The filling came out when I was cleaning my teeth and unfortunately I couldn't go to the dentist.
7a. The windscreen shattered while I was driving to work, but fortunately there was no traffic behind me.
7b. The windscreen shattered while I was driving to work and unfortunately I was a long way from a telephone.
8a. The kettle exploded when I was boiling some water, but fortunately nobody was injured.
8b. The kettle exploded when I was boiling some water and unfortunately I was right next to it.

5 How many words?

1. I met them at the station.
2. She went for a walk in the lane.
3. He got out of the car and shut the door.
4. While we were leaving, a cat ran into the house.
5. I was working when they arrived.
6. They left a couple of days ago.
7. I went to visit them after the match.
8. I got a lovely present for my birthday.

7 A poem

Why I didn't send you a birthday card
Because I've lost your address
because I don't believe in
        birthdays
because I like to be
        different
because I forgot.

13 IT'S BETTER TO TRAVEL THAN TO ARRIVE

3 I want some information

1. I asked her for information. *or* I asked her for some information.
2. We'll need a lot of equipment.
3. How much luggage have you got?
4. It's wonderful news.
5. He gave me some advice.
6. We had wonderful weather.
7. Unfortunately I got flu on holiday.
8. We had some trouble at the airport.

6 The last minute

1. Andrew:
Well, I always check the windows carefully before I leave home on a long journey, and of course, I call and see my neighbour in the next flat to give her my key and say goodbye. I check that the gas is turned off too. I quite often go round all the rooms, just looking in the room to remember what it is like, make sure I haven't forgotten anything Oh, yes, of course, I always go the the bathroom last thing!

2. Patti:
LYNN: Patti, before you go away on a long journey, abroad or wherever, what are the things that you normally do just before you leave?
PATTI: Well, I must admit that I never remember to do some of the important things, like, I never turn off the gas, and I never remember to unplug all the electrical appliances, and I never remember to turn off the water. Um, I'm very good with safety and security, so I do remember to check that the windows are locked and, er, I check and double check to see that I've got my passport and my tickets, and I usually walk from room to room to make sure that I haven't forgotten anything. I draw the curtains, um, and then I usually go next door and tell the neighbour that I'm going to be away for a while, and could they just watch the house.
LYNN: If you have anything valuable, do you make an effort to hide it, or …
PATTI: Yes, usually. Oh, and I always go to the toilet. That's the last thing I do, because I know if I don't, I'll regret it.

14 POSSESSIONS

2 Past participles

drive: I've driven it.
wash: I've washed it.
use: I've used it.
buy: I've bought it.
carry: I've carried it.
win: I've won it.
read: I've read it.
write: I've written it.
feed: I've fed it.
start: I've started it.
wear: I've worn it.
learn: I've learnt it.
have: I've had it.

5 Problems with electrical appliances

SPEAKER 1: I always seem to lose the guarantee, so that when the appliance goes wrong, if it does, I can never find it because I've put it in such a safe place that I've forgotten where it was.

SPEAKER 2: Lots of electrical appliances that you buy in Britain come without a plug, and I always spend ages fitting a plug on the appliance because I'm very bad at that sort of thing.

SPEAKER 3: I don't know how to programme my new video. I was all right with the old one, but this is a new one which is run by remote control and, well, I just don't understand it at all.

SPEAKER 4: They always claim that the assembly of the electrical appliance is simple, but so often the instructions have been translated from another language and they're very difficult to follow.

SPEAKER 5: My problem is I never read the instructions. I always assume I know how to put it together, so I'll start putting it together, the whole thing doesn't work, I take it back to the shops, and they fix it for me.

SPEAKER 6: I went to buy some batteries for my camera the other day, and bought completely the wrong size. I thought I knew what size they were, but obviously I hadn't really looked.

15 RULES

5 Good and bad language rules

The first rule is correct. We do use *who* to refer to people. When we refer to things we use *that* or *which*.

The second rule is also correct, but the third rule is completely wrong. The letter *k* is not pronounced if the next letter is *n* – for example *knee* or *knife*. It is pronounced if the next letter is anything else – for example, *kind*.

Rule four is correct – *mathematics*, *politics* and *news* are all used with singular verbs, and the fifth rule is also true. *Pleased to meet you* is used when we meet people in formal situations, along with the other phrase *How do you do?* Both are common.

Rule six is another that is correct, but rule seven is wrong. In English we do use the present continuous to talk about the future. When we are talking about things we have arranged with others, for example, we can say, *We're having dinner with friends tomorrow evening* or *I'm seeing the dentist at 3.30 this afternoon*.

And rule eight is also wrong. After *must* you don't use *to*. For example, *I must go home*, or *We must finish early*. The same applies to other important modal verbs such as *can* and *may*.

And finally rule nine. Yes, this is also wrong. Nouns may have the main stress on any syllable. Think about these: *cinema* – first syllable, but *decision* – that's the second syllable; *education* – that's the third syllable; *pronunciation* – that's the fourth syllable.

However, it is generally true to say that if a noun has three syllables or more, the stress is not usually on the last syllable. There are exceptions, but not too many. If you are not sure about the stress, look in a dictionary. You will find that dictionaries mark the stressed syllable where they also show the word written in phonetics. Sometimes they underline the stressed syllable and sometimes they put a little mark before the stressed syllable.

16 KEEPING THE CUSTOMER SATISFIED

3 Syllables and word stress

Words with the main stress on the first syllable:
opposite
message
Wednesday
business
suitable
Words with the main stress on the second syllable:
experience
research
reliable
economist
polite
appearance
Words with the main stress on the third syllable:
questionnaire
competition
vegetarian

7 What does she think?

Well I think that the population might possibly rise by, um, I don't know maybe three or four per cent. I think possibly life expectancy for woman will rise actually. For men I'm not really so sure ... I think it probably won't rise very much at all. Retirement, um, I don't think really will come down a great deal. Possibly, um, maybe, that for men it might be 60, I think the women will still stay at 60.

I think our diets will change actually quite a bit because they are already. People are eating more fish and fruit and vegetables, and less red meat and, er, fats, cheese, etc.

Um, I think maybe we will spend a bit more on clothes and possibly on appearances. Um, not a great deal but I think maybe just a little bit more.

Regarding shops, I think, um, yes, they will be located outside of towns because shopping centres seem to be the thing now, so I think that, um, that might well be true that people will shop outside, um, the towns. Also, um, shopping from home, um, ordering things from catalogues, I think that might get bigger now because it seems to be happening quite a bit.

Um, regarding leisure, I think people will watch television more because there seem to be so many more channels now with, um, Sky television and cable television coming in. Um, foreign travel I think is definitely going up all the time and that certainly will increase.

Eating out I think is getting more and more popular since people travel so much, um, I think that will certainly rise.

17 PICTURE THIS!

3 Word partnerships

1. People who always make mistakes are careless.
2. People who always tell the truth are honest.
3. People who always take taxis are lazy.
4. People who tell lies are dishonest.
5. People who make appointments and then break them are unreliable.
6. People who always make a lot of noise are irritating.
7. People who tell amusing stories are funny.
8. People who never do anyone a favour are mean.

5 Photo in St James Park

a hot spring day by the lake
and a young woman and man
probably tourists
possibly Spanish
who wanted a photo of themselves together
handed their camera to someone
almost definitely English
who certain fellow countrymen
might predictably describe
as a very drunken old dosser
but to them he was just a passer-by
he accepted the camera
took a long time focusing
and steadying himself
but managed to take the picture
and received genuine gratitude
from the two
who had seen nothing deviant in his behaviour
and who would remember him
as a friendly and helpful
English gentleman
if he hadn't fallen into the lake
with their camera.

18 LISTS

1 Could you lend me some money?

1.
A: Would you like to go out this evening?
B: Yes, I'd love to.

2.
A: How about next Tuesday?
B: Yeah, that's fine.

3.
A: Could you lend me some money?
B: Yes, of course. How much do you want?

4.
A: I think you should phone the police.
B: Yeah, that's a good idea.

5.
A: I'm sorry I'm late.
B: Never mind, don't worry.

6.
A: Oh, that's very kind of you.
B: Not at all.

7.
A: I intend to start a new business next year.
B: Really. That'll be interesting.

8.
A: I'm late because the traffic was terrible.
B: That's OK, don't worry.

3 Lexical sets

1. He told me just to bring a knife, fork and spoon.
2. She was wearing flat shoes, a brown skirt and a white blouse.
3. You can get these jackets in cotton, suede or leather.
4. They only sell three sizes: small, medium or large.
5. The hotel said they could provide bed and breakfast, half board or full board.
6. It's a fixed-price menu, and you get a starter, a main course and a dessert.
7. They ask people not to smoke cigarettes, pipes or cigars.
8. It was a fairly typical bathroom: a bath, shower, toilet and washbasin.

9. She won three medals at the Olympics: a gold, a silver and a bronze.
10. I had the hearts, and she had the clubs, spades and diamonds.

7 A list of facts

Well, first of all the *Vittoria*, that's a sailing ship, took two years to do it – that was between 1519 and 1521. Then there's the USS *Triton*, a nuclear submarine, which took 2 months and 25 days in 1960. Before that, in 1929, the *Graf Zeppelin*, an airship, took 21 days, 7 hours and 34 minutes. Five years earlier an aircraft called *Chicago* did it in 14 days, 15 hours and 11 minutes.

In 1957 a Boeing B–52 took one day, 21 hours and 19 minutes, and finally there is *Cosmos l69*, a satellite, which did it in 80 minutes and 30.6 seconds in 1967. Now that's an interesting set of facts, isn't it? What do you think it's about?

19 PUT YOUR TRUST IN OTHERS

7 Offers and requests

1. Excuse me. Could I borrow your pen?
2. Would you like a lift to the station?
3. Could you give me a hand with this suitcase?
4. Could I have a look at your paper for a minute?
5. Would you like something to eat?
6. Would you like to keep it?
7. Do you think you could open the window?
8. Would you like some help?
9. Do you think you could lend me the money?
10. Do you think I could change the appointment?

20 THE SENSES

4 Listen and answer

1. Is furniture polish something you can eat?
2. Is mud pleasant to walk in?
3. Are cherries a kind of fruit?
4. Is glue something you use in an office?
5. Does velvet feel soft?
6. Does garlic smell like chocolate?
7. Is marble harder than sand?
8. Can you put perfume behind your ears?
9. Can you wash things in soap powder?
10. Do you put ink in a camera?
11. Can you eat a lorry?
12. Does leather smell like paint?
13. Does fur taste nice?
14. Is snakeskin something you can drink?
15. Does a lift go up and down?

5 Odd one out

1. snake   banana   favourite   taste
   So *banana* is the odd one out.
2. honey   mud   lovely   nylon
   So *nylon* is the odd one out.
3. speak   leather   pleasant   instead
   So *speak* is the odd one out.
4. lamb   salmon   orange   sand
   So *orange* is the odd one out.
5. forest   strong   cotton   smoke
   So *smoke* is the odd one out.
6. worse   Norway   burn   fur
   So *Norway* is the odd one out.

7 Writing a story together

WOMAN: In this activity, we are going to develop a story together. Sometimes you have to write down what is said, sometimes you invent part of the story yourself. If you hear a ping like this (PING), stop the recording, and work until you are ready to start again and continue the story. If you hear a man's voice, you need to write down exactly what he says. If you hear my voice, you need to follow the instruction. Listen more than once, if necessary.

MAN: We arrived at the little café, late at night, just before closing time. It was raining hard and we were tired and thirsty after our long journey. Someone in the village told us about the café, which was the only place open at this time of night. As we walked in, we could see ...

WOMAN: Now, what could you see? Complete the sentence yourself, describing the scene.

MAN: We moved over to the bar, and ordered coffee and sandwiches We could smell ...

WOMAN: What could you smell? Think of two or three things, then choose the best, and write it down.

MAN: Suddenly, there was a noise outside the door.

WOMAN: What could you hear? What happened because of the noise? Finish the story.

WOMAN: If you like, compare your story to your speaking partner's.

21 TIME

4 At three o'clock in the morning

WOMAN:
1. I was born at 12.15 in 1960.
2. I started school in October.
3. I usually go on a holiday in August, perhaps July.
4. I always clean my teeth in the morning.
5. I usually leave the house in the morning at around 9.30, 10. I like to avoid the rushhour.
6. I sometimes go to parties at night, but I prefer to stay home.
7. I sometimes go for long walks in winter.
8. My last lesson was so long ago I can't remember.
9. I take my clothes off every night.
10. We have a national holiday on Christmas Day.

MAN:
1. I was born at about 9.30 in the morning on a Friday in 1957.
2. I started school in September when I was four and a half.
3. I usually go on holiday in the summer I suppose, I mean I like it to be warm.
4. I always clean my teeth at night and in the morning.
5. I usually leave the house in the morning at 9 o'clock, depending on where I'm going.
6. I sometimes go to parties in the afternoon, not so much at night.
7. I sometimes go for long walks on a Sunday.
8. My last lesson was a class that I did in November.
9. I take my clothes off at night.
10. We have a national holiday on the first of May.

7 How do you spend your time?

1. When was the last time you wrote a cheque for a large amount of money?
2. When will you next go for a long walk?
3. When did you last catch a bus?
4. When will you next go out to a restaurant?
5. When did you last ride a bike?
6. When did you last deposit some money in your bank account?
7. When did you last have a haircut?

8. When will you next see your English teacher?
9. When did you last have a really good sleep?
10. When did you last have to cancel a ticket?
11. When will you next spend a lot of money?
12. When will you next see your best friend?
13. When did you last write in a diary?
14. When did you last see a calendar?
15. When will you next speak English?

22 A SENSE OF HISTORY

5 Word stress

die; death
elect; election
murder; murder
explode; explosion
escape; escape
develop; development
invade; invasion
assassinate; assassination
win; win
invent; invention
resign; resignation
destroy; destruction

7 Dictation

1a. The fire destroyed the building.
1b. It started in one of the bedrooms.
2a. The man saw the thief.
2b. He lives on the other side of the street.
3a. The accident was on the front page of the newspaper.
3b. It happened near our house.
4a. The boy used to steal my apples.
4b. He later became a policeman.

23 WHOSE LIFE IS IT ANYWAY?

1 What do you call them?

Joumana

I call my friends by their first names, and I call my doctor by his title. I call my teacher Mary, and I usually call my boss by his first name. My landlady, I always call her by her surname – she's quite a bit older than me and she's rather a formal sort of person. I call my dentist Mrs Patterson, and I don't call a stranger in the street anything. I don't call my tax inspector anything either – in fact I'd rather not speak to him at all. Um, I don't call a waiter anything, and my grandparents I call Gran and Grandpa. I, um, call my newspaper seller Arun – I know him quite well – but I call my bank manager by her surname. My parents I call Mum and Dad, most of the time.

Stefan

I call my friends by their first names, and I call my doctor by his title. I call my teacher Mr Curran, and I call my boss by his surname.
I call my landlord by his first name and I call my dentist by his title. I, I don't call a stranger in the street anything. I call ... I don't call the tax inspector anything. And I call a waiter in the restaurant with 'Excuse me, please'. I call my grandparents, um, Grandma and Grandpa. I don't call my newspaper seller anything. I call my bank manager Mrs Wetherall, and I call my parents Ma and Pa.

4 Sounds and spelling

choose; unusual
such; culture
spider; rhyme
brain; strange
joke; so
common; politics
call; report
surname; prefer

6 Expressing preferences

1. Shall we practise listening?
2. Shall we go to the laboratory?
3. Shall we do a test?
4. Shall we do some pronunciation practice?
5. Shall we revise some expressions?
6. Shall we practise the present perfect?
7. Shall we work in groups?

24 CINEMA AND THE ARTS

4 First names in English

Names that have the sound /iː/:
Sheila
Stephen
Jean
Leo
Neil
Names that have the sound /uː/:
Andrew
Stewart
Julia
Judy
Names that have the sound /ɔː/:
Paul
Lorna
George
Laura
Names that have the sound /əʊ/:
Joan
Rose

6 Playing in a band

SPENCER:

Well, as you know, I play in a group. It's actually called Broken Glass, which is about the fourth different name we've had. And we started up about five years ago, just after I moved to London, although the other guys have lived here all their lives. There are four of us altogether: Robin plays guitar and flute, Mike also plays guitar, I'm on piano and keyboards and Doug is our drummer.

Describing the type of music we play is kind of difficult. I actually studied music at university, and I'm influenced by all sorts of things – jazz, rock, classical, you name it. Doug is just an old-fashioned drummer who likes really heavy rock music. And Mike and Robin will play just about anything. I guess, though, that you'd call most of our stuff sort of gentle rock music. We do other people's songs some of the time, but Robin now writes most of the stuff we play.

As to where we perform, that's just about anywhere, if someone pays us. Most of the time it's in music pubs, but we also do quite a few private parties.

If we're very busy, either at work, or if we have lots of gigs, we don't have much time for practice. But we try to get together once a week in the evening, and we usually manage that, though it may only be for an hour or so, but it helps.

ANSWER KEY

1 GETTING STARTED

1 He's making a movie

1. b, c, a
2. c, b, a
3. b, c, a
4. a, c, b
5. c, b, a
6. c, a, b

2 I come from Stockholm

1. I come from Sweden, but I am living in Cambridge at the moment, because I am doing an English course at a language school. I am staying with an English family who live just outside the city centre.
I work for a large company which makes sports equipment.

2. I am saving up to do a language course in the United States next year because I work in advertising, and almost everyone in this business speaks English. At the moment, I am doing an evening course, just three hours a week, but I've got an American friend, who I meet regularly, and we always speak English to each other.

3 There's a mistake – it should be ...

mistake	*correction*
1.	(it should be)
In my desk	On my desk
lamp table	table lamp
birthday's	birthday
Some times	Sometimes
too much	too many
in my desk	on my desk
2.	
His	It is/It's
think	thing
in my right	on my right
write always	always write
two dictionary	two dictionaries
a lot water	a lot of water

5 Understanding this book

A

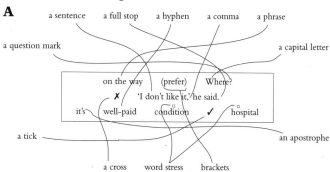

B

comprehension – understanding
complete – fill in
wrong – incorrect
record – written description
false – not true
choose – select
omit – leave out
correct – right

6 Correct the text

I went to a fortune-teller once**.** His name was Mr **Chatterjee**; he had a small shop between a pastry-maker's and a silk-dealer, in the middle of the bazaar, in Delhi.
It was not my idea to consult Mr **Chatterjee**. I did not believe in fortune-tellers, horoscopes, **T**arot cards or any of that kind of thing. Nor did my friend Wexton, but he was always full of surprises and when he suggested that I go, I thought: *Why not?*
'Won't you come too**,** Wexton?' I said. 'He could read both our fortunes.' Wexton smiled.
'At my age,' he replied, 'you don**'**t need a fortune-teller to predict your future, Victoria.'

7 Writers and their work routines

A

Russell Hoban

I usually *get up* at about eight thirty or nine o'clock, and after breakfast I come to my desk. I suppose I am a creature of habit because I have a very strict *routine*. First, I cross off yesterday on the *calendar*, then I write in my *diary* what I did yesterday. After that, I select my music for the day, and I make a *copy* of what I wrote the day *before* on my word processor.

Jessie Kesson

I bought an *antique* armchair and I sit there every day to write. I need cigarettes and lots of cups of tea or coffee. Some days, I get up as *early* as four thirty; that gives me time to think. I go back and read what I wrote the *previous* day.
My pencil is almost part of myself – I write everything *by hand*. I can't *type*, and in any case, I certainly couldn't write straight onto a typewriter. I couldn't think of the words. Words are *ugly* things and hard to work with.

B

1. Sally Beauman, Jessie Kesson
2. Sally Beauman
3. Russell Hoban
4. Jessie Kesson
5. Russell Hoban
6. Sally Beauman
7. Jeffrey Archer

9 Visual dictionary

1. bookcase   2. photocopier   3. word processor
4. filing cabinet   5. chair   6. briefcase
7. wastepaper bin   8. file   9. notebook   10. hole
punch   11. stapler   12. ruler   13. scissors
14. pencil sharpener   15. rubber   16. sheet of paper
17. calculator   18. ballpoint pen   19. desk

2 ASKING QUESTIONS

1 Jumbled questions

1. Where did she grow up?
2. Why don't you visit them?
3. Are people in your profession well-paid?
   Are people well-paid in your profession?
4. Who do you vote for?
5. Do you know where the station is?
6. What is your flat like?
7. How much do you spend each month?
8. What type of building is it?
9. Are you interested in politics?
10. How much do you earn?

2 What, where and how often?

A

1. Where   2. When   3. How   4. Whose
5. Which   6. How far   7. How long   8. What
9. How often   10. Why

3 Opposites and contrasts

1. badly   2. lazy   3. failed   4. easy   5. boring
6. stayed   7. hated   8. unemployed / out of work

5 Stress and rhythm

1. When did you first meet him?
2. Where did you meet her?
3. How often do you see them?
4. How far is it to her house?
5. Why do you like her?
6. When did you last see him?
7. How often do you phone them?
8. Why did you leave him?

6 Kangaroos

B

Here are some possible questions. If you didn't write some of the questions below, don't worry. You probably already know the answers!

1. How long do kangaroos live?
2. Why are they called kangaroos?
3. How fast can they hop?
4. How far can they jump?
5. How high can they jump?
6. Why do they hop?
7. How tall are they?
8. What do they weigh?
9. What enemies do they have?
10. Where do they live?
11. How long do babies live in the pouch?
12. Are they friendly to humans?
13. How many kinds of kangaroos are there?
14. Do they live in groups?
15. Which countries do they live in?
16. Do people eat their meat?
17. Is it true that they box?

Now go back to page 11; don't look at the answers below yet.

1. Average 15; maximum 30. (Reading)
2. When Captain Cook asked the Aborigines what the animals were, they replied 'kangaroo'. He took that to be their name, although 'kangaroo' actually meant 'I don't know' in their language. (Listening)
3. Up to 60 kilometres per hour. (Reading)
4. 1.5 – 3 metres; maximum 6 metres. (Reading)
5. 3 metres. (Reading)
6. It's easier to carry babies if they stay upright and hop. (Listening)
7. Up to 2 metres. (Reading)
8. Up to 90 kilograms. (Reading)
9. Large birds of prey, large lizards, snakes, dingoes, humans. (Listening)
10. Grassland and open forest. (Reading)
11. Six months. (Reading)
12. Quite friendly but also timid. (Listening)
13. 40. (Reading)
14. Yes. (Listening)
15. Australia, Tasmania and New Guinea. (Reading)
16. Yes. (Listening)
17. Yes. (Listening)

8 Jokes

a – 3   b – 4   c – 5   d – 2   e – 1

3 STREETLIFE

1 Take the first road on the left

Take the	first road	on the left.
	second street	on the right.
	third turning	

Go straight on,	until	you get to	the hospital.
ahead,		come to	the main road.
Keep going,			the roundabout.

| It's on the | left-hand | side of the | road. |
| | right-hand | | street. |

It's	opposite	the bank.
	next to	
	near	
	behind	

Turn	right	at the bank.
	left	at the museum.
		into the main road.

It's just	after	the post office.
	before	the library.
	next to	the bank.

2 It might be Chinese

1. Japanese   2. Portuguese   3. Thai   4. Russian
5. Chinese   6. Spanish   7. Dutch   8. Arabic
9. Urdu   10. Swahili   11. Hebrew

3 Picture dictation

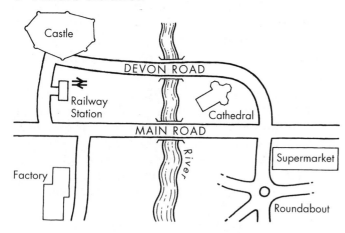

4 Dialogues

1. the cathedral; Thank you very much.
2. the castle
3. Yes. Go down to the main road, turn left, take the first turning on the right and the factory is at the end of the road.
4. Excuse me. Could you tell me where the supermarket is?; Thanks a lot/very much.
5. I'm sorry, I've no idea.

5 Unusual maps

1. B   2. C   3. A   4. D

6 A bad sense of direction

	Gareth	Lynn	Ian
Who were they with?	colleagues	family	group of friends
Where did they get lost?	San Antonio, Texas	wood in Dartmoor	on a hill
Why did they get lost?	they missed a turn-off	no map	bad weather
How long were they lost?	1½ hours	1 hour	2 hours

7 Postcards

Dear Jack,

It'll be great to see you next week, and it's very easy to get to the house. <u>Take</u> the 57 bus from the station and <u>get off</u> at the market. Then <u>go</u> along Kendall Street until you <u>get</u> to the post office. <u>Turn</u> left and my road is the second on the right. See you at eight o'clock.

9 Visual dictionary

1. over/above   2. under/below   3. between
4. next to   5. near   6. behind   7. in front of
8. opposite   9. along   10. past   11. through

12. up   13. on / on top (of)   14. down
15. towards   16. into   17. out of   18. among

4 CREATIVITY

1 Missing letters

1. He hasn't been abroad in his life.
2. She wasn't at home yesterday.
3. Has anyone ever used a brick as a paperweight?
4. She didn't go out last night.
5. I've never made a speech in public.
6. Were you busy last week?
7. Have you ever played football with an orange?
8. We haven't seen any good films here.
9. Who wrote the words for that song?
10. He has made some beautiful ornaments.

2 Dictation

See tapescript on page 133.

3 Expressing personal feelings

B
1. e   2. a   3. d   4. c   5. f   6. b

4 Creative word search

breakfast: ate, are, bake, bar, bare, bear, beast, brake, break, breast, ear, east, eat, fake, far, fare, fast, fear, feast, rat, rate, safe, stake, star, stare, steak, tear.

calendar: ace, ale, are, can, cane, car, card, care, clean, clear, dare, deal, dear, lace, land, lane, lead, led, lend, race, ran, read, real, red.

5 Weak vowels and word stress

angry   /ˈæŋgrɪ/
confused   /kənˈfjuːzd/
embarrassed   /ɪmˈbærəst/
umbrella   /ʌmˈbrelə/
Japan   /dʒəˈpæn/
connect   /kəˈnekt/
apologise   /əˈpɒlədʒaɪz/
collar   /ˈkɒlə/
panic   /ˈpænɪk/
comma   /ˈkɒmə/

8 Creative uses

Possible answers:
A
You can use a blanket:
as a curtain; on the floor, as a rug; to dry yourself after a shower; to hide something.
You can use a bowl:
as a plant pot; as an ornament; to put food in; to catch a spider; to catch water when it leaks from a pipe; as an aquarium, to keep fish in.

B

a. funny ending:
… but unfortunately his leg knocked against the table and a large bowl of ice-cream fell off the edge and onto a lady sitting in front of him.
b. happy ending:
… and told the people that the war was over, and that he would lead the country into a new era of peace and prosperity. The audience cheered and cheered.
c. shocking ending:
… and began with these words: 'I am sorry to have to tell you that my doctors have told me I am a dying man, and so this will be my last speech as your leader.'

5 YOU AND YOUR BODY

1 Break, broke, broken

Infinitive	*Past tense*	*Past participle*
break	broke	broken
feel	felt	felt
hurt	hurt	hurt
shake	shook	shaken
cut	cut	cut
bend	bent	bent
throw	threw	thrown
give	gave	given
take	took	taken
teach	taught	taught
spend	spent	spent
bring	brought	brought
find	found	found
know	knew	known
lie (on a bed)	lay	lain

2 Enjoy yourself

1. herself   2. ourselves   3. myself   4. themselves
5. yourself   6. ourselves   7. himself   8. myself

3 How often do you …?

A

Box A
1. quite often
2. sometimes
3. occasionally
4. hardly ever
5. never

Box B
1. twice a day
2. every day
3. every other day
4. once a week
5. every couple of months
6. three times a year

4 I shut my head

1. I shook my head.
2. I combed my hair.
3. I took my vitamin pills.
4. I pointed my finger at him.
5. I folded my arms.
6. I did yoga.
7. I shut my eyes.
8. I ran upstairs.
9. I had a cold.
10. I felt ill.

6 When I was in Spain …

Where and when it happened:

This is about an accident that happened when I was in Spain.

Information about the situation:

One day I parked my car outside a shop and got out.

Sequence of events in the story:

Just at that moment, I saw a friend across the street. As I said 'hello', I shut my finger in the door. It was badly cut and terribly painful. My friend rushed over and drove me to the hospital, where they cleaned and bandaged my finger.

Result of the events:

Incredibly, I still have the scar today, fifteen years later.

8 Visual dictionary

1. finger   2. thumb   3. nail   4. toes   5. elbow
6. waist   7. wrist   8. shoulder   9. lip   10. knee
11. heel   12. chin   13. eyebrow   14. neck
15. ankle

6 LEARNING – PAST AND PRESENT

1 *I've seen or I saw?*

1. 've seen
2. saved; 've spent
3. gave
4. 've been
5. spoke
6. got; haven't seen
7. have had
8. came; haven't eaten
9. 've done
10. bought; was; 've had
11. haven't travelled; had
12. 've received

2 Words with more than one meaning

3 It's such an easy exercise

A

1. such   2. such   3. so   4. such   5. so   6. such
7. so   8. so

B

Possible answers:

1. It was so dark/foggy
   It was such a dark/foggy night
2. She was so happy
3. It was so horrible/frightening/disgusting
   It was such a horrible film
4. I was so angry
   It was such a bad product
5. I was so shocked/surprised
6. It was so noisy
   There was such a lot of noise
7. I was so tired
8. It was such a good game/match
   The game was so good

4 How to pronounce the letter *u*

/ʌ/	/uː/ or	/juː/
sun	true	tube
subject	rule	useless
lunch		computer
just		student
sunny		use
adult		refuse
such		confused
unpleasant		
study		
discuss		

8 *Writing, writting, or writeing?*

1. I'm *writing* to tell you about my *travelling* arrangements.
2. They *offered* him a lot of money for the car.
3. We are *planning* to go *swimming* next week. Are you *coming*?
4. They *cancelled* the show because a lot of people were ill.
5. The man *robbed* the bank, but then dropped the money when he climbed over a wall. Later he was *stopped* by the police.
6. I'm hoping to go next week, but I'm not *taking* the car because the roads are always so busy.
7. She has *forgotten* her key again.
8. Why are you *using* my dictionary?
9. He *admitted* it was his mistake.
10. When I phoned her she *promised* to help.

7 LETTERS THAT TELL A STORY

1 Lexical pairs

street; motorway
tent; caravan
hepatitis; sore throat
adult; teenager
lemons; oranges
knife; gun
lake; pond
word processor; typewriter
fortnight; week
dustman; dentist

2 A leopard is faster than a camel

See tapescript on page 133 for possible answers.

3 Prefixes

A

insensitive   informal   dishonest   unpopular
disorganised   unimaginative   unexpected   illegible
unfriendly   unreliable   unsatisfactory   illegal

B

1. unpopular   6. unsatisfactory
2. dishonest   7. illegal
3. insensitive   8. unexpected
4. unreliable   9. disorganised
5. illegible   10. informal

4 Text types

recipe: add flour; one small onion, chopped
diary entry: ring vet; plumber 10.30 am; dental appointment
postcard: lovely weather; see you soon; airmail
application form: marital status; occupation
addressed envelope: Private and Confidential; urgent; airmail
formal letter: Yours faithfully; We apologise for the delay

5 What do your letters say?

1. c   2. e   3. b   4. f   5. g   6. h   7. a   8. d

6 Learning to write

Lynn

1. 4.
2. capitals easier than small letters; couldn't use pens, had to use pencils.
3. a few characters in Chinese.
4. easy to read, quite good.
5. quite impressive.

Gareth

1. 5.
2. neatly on two lines; wooden pens and ink; be careful about ink blots.
3. a bit of Old Testament Greek (has forgotten it).
4. almost illegible.
5. rather good.

7 Spelling rules

A

3. fat	fatter	the fattest
4. small	smaller	the smallest
5. neat	neater	the neatest
6. thin	thinner	the thinnest
7. wet	wetter	the wettest
8. cheap	cheaper	the cheapest

B

1. easy	easier	the easiest
2. busy	busier	the busiest
3. tidy	tidier	the tidiest
4. funny	funnier	the funniest
5. lively	livelier	the liveliest
6. cloudy	cloudier	the cloudiest
7. happy	happier	the happiest
8. sunny	sunnier	the sunniest
9. heavy	heavier	the heaviest
10. foggy	foggier	the foggiest

8 TAKE IT OR LEAVE IT

1 Are you busy this evening?

1. I'm meeting / I'm going to meet; I'm going to watch; I'll do.
2. He's doing / he's going to do; she's staying / she's going to stay; she's going to do / she's doing; I'm meeting / I'm going to meet; I'll have; I'll call.
3. Bill and Pam are opening / Bill and Pam are going to open; I'm having / I'm going to have; I'll give.

2 Could you ring me back?

1. took   2. pay   3. be   4. bring   5. ring
6. have   7. go   8. come   9. sent   10. put

3 Paraphrasing

1. don't fit (very well)
2. take it back to the shop
3. something wrong
4. took my clothes off
5. my money back
6. is the changing room / fitting room
7. a receipt
8. afraid
9. you lend me
10. health care

4 Sounds familiar

See tapescript on page 134.

5 Shopping in London

Bartholdi: lamb chops
Kiku: chopsticks
Divertimenti: a frying pan
Turak: a necklace
Inca: a scarf
Deliss: a pair of sandals

7 Skeleton story

(*Some slight variation possible*)
I saw some / a pair of trousers and decided to try them on. I paid in cash and got a receipt. When I took them home, I discovered there was a problem with them. I took them back to the shop and asked for a refund. The assistant wanted to see my receipt. She/He gave me my/the money back immediately.

9 Visual dictionary

1. blouse   2. skirt   3. sweater/jumper   4. trousers
5. gloves   6. scarf   7. raincoat   8. tie   9. shirt
10. belt   11. jacket   12. suit   13 turn on
14. turn off   15. turn up   16. turn down
17. put on   18. take off   19. try on

9 FOOD AND DRINK

1 Correct my mistakes

1. is usually served
2. is often drunk
3. is made from
4. are drunk
5. is served
6. is not normally grown
7. is exported
8. are sold

2 Dialogue completion

1. have to / must; don't have to
2. should; shouldn't/mustn't
3. don't have to
4. mustn't
5. mustn't/shouldn't
6. have to/must

3 Verbs with two objects

A
1. The customer ordered the meal.
2. The chef cooked the customer a steak.
3. The waiter brought the customer the first course.
4. The waiter served the customer the main course.
5. The waiter poured the customer a glass of wine.
6. The waiter offered the customer a dessert from the trolley.
7. The waiter gave the customer the bill.
8. The customer paid the bill and left the waiter a tip.

B
Possible answers:
1. He cooked a meal for twenty people.
2. I showed the pictures to my wife.
3. She poured some wine for her guests.
4. They gave the money to their children.
5. I offered the job to the young woman.
6. We left a tip for the waiter.
7. I sent the tickets to my boss.
8. He served the food to the customers at the end table.

4 Food

1. Strawberries are heart-shaped; peaches are round; grapes can be green or black.
2. Peppers, avocado, lettuce, cucumber, beans, grapes and cabbage are all green.
3. You can't eat the peel of avocado, mango, pineapple, garlic or onion. In some countries also peaches, cucumber and grapes.
4. Fish, lobster, bacon, ham, lamb, duck, pork and snails were all living creatures.
5. You can read a menu, a recipe and a bill.
6. You eat with a knife, fork, spoon and cutlery.
7. Starter, main course and dessert are all parts of a meal.

Mustard is the only word left.

5 Tourist guides

1. Japan   2. France   3. Holland   4. Colombia

6 What's on the menu?

See tapescript on page 134.

7 Sequencing events

An Evening Out
It was a lovely evening. First we went to an Italian restaurant for a quick pizza. Then we went to the cinema to see the latest film starring Kevin Costner. After that we had a couple of drinks in a bar, and then finally we went back to Joao's flat to listen to some music.

9 Visual dictionary

1. melon   2. peaches   3. pineapple   4. pears
5. strawberries   6. avocado   7. grapes   8. rice
9. potatoes   10. carrots   11. lettuce   12. cucumber
13. peppers   14. mushrooms   15. parsley
16. cabbage   17. onions   18. aubergines
19. cauliflower   20. beans   21. peas   22. garlic
23. prawns   24. crab   25. lobster   26. mussels
27. snails

10 FEELINGS: THE GOOD, THE BAD AND THE UGLY

1 Make a suggestion

2. She could feed the dog.
   She could complain to the neighbours.
3. He could swim after the oar.
   He could shout for help.
4. She could take a sleeping pill.
   She could read a book.
5. He could make another cake.
   He could cut the burnt bits off.
6. She could call the fire brigade.
   She could fetch a ladder.
7. He could say it wasn't his suitcase.
   He could say he is a watch salesman.

2 Using *get*

A

get (= to buy) something to eat; a washing machine.
get (= to become) depressed; tired; annoyed.
get (= to receive) a letter, a phone call; a bill.
get (= to catch/develop an illness) flu; hepatitis.
get (= to obtain) a driving licence; some money from the bank.

B

1. a phone call   2. tired   3. driving licence
4. something to eat   5. annoyed   6. bill   7. flu
8. depressed

3 What did they say?

1. She gave up smoking a year ago.
2. He intends to go to California in the summer.
3. She said she enjoyed seeing Bill.
4. He decided to take a taxi because he was late.
5. She can't stand getting up early.
6. She regrets leaving school at 16.
7. He doesn't mind walking if necessary.
8. I try to avoid going to work when the traffic is bad.

4 Sounds missing

See tapescript on page 134.

6 Do you like blue?

1. physical exercise: quite happy and fit
2. chocolate: warm inside
3. cool beer: refreshed
4. rock music: old
5. wine: very sociable
6. the colour green: rested and relaxed
7. raw egg: quite sick
8. hot weather: very bad-tempered
9. public transport: so angry I could scream
10. the colour blue: calm and relaxed
11. birthdays: like I'm a child again

7 Dear Abby ...

making; being; living; listening; watching; doing; to give up; to marry; to get; to hear.

9 Visual dictionary

1. start a car   2. tell a joke   3. do homework
4. look at a photo   5. make a cake   6. have a sauna
7. watch a film   8. do the housework
9. give up smoking   10. dig the garden
11. listen to a story   12. take a photo
13. walk the dog

11 WEATHER

1 What's it like?

Adjectives: climatic; sunny; windy; cloudy; foggy; showery; icy; misty; thundery
Nouns: humidity; heat; cold

2 Quantity

A

1. enough   2. too   3. enough   4. too many
5. enough   6. too much   7. too many   8. too
9. too much   10. too many

B

Possible answers:

English grammar is too difficult.

I have too much work to do.

I make too many mistakes when I speak.

I miss too many lessons because I am very busy.

My pronunciation isn't good enough.

I don't study hard enough.

I haven't got enough books.

There are too many students in my class.

I don't have enough friends who speak English.

During class I speak my first language too much.

3 Hot and cold countries

Important in hot countries:

suntan lotion; fans; T-shirts; short-sleeved shirts; soft drinks; air conditioning; ice cubes

Important in cold countries:

blankets; umbrellas; gloves; woollen scarves; boots; socks; overcoats; central heating

4 Learning English keeps me busy

Possible answers:

Regular exercise keeps you fit / in good condition / healthy.

An electric blanket keeps you warm (at night).

A positive attitude to life keeps you healthy/young/happy.

An umbrella stops you getting wet.

Too much noise stops you sleeping / getting to sleep.

Tranquillisers stop you getting worried or anxious.

Drinking wine can be bad for your liver / can be very relaxing.

Smoking can kill you / be dangerous to your health / damage your lungs.

Sleeping pills can help you sleep better / be useful / be addictive.

5 Using the weather to predict the future

A

Missing words in sayings:

1. Red sky *in the morning*
2. Clear before *eleven.*
3. Short notice, *soon past.*
4. Winter is gone and won't come *again.*

B

Saying 1: some truth

Saying 2: a bit of truth

Saying 3: a lot of truth

Saying 4: not much truth at all

6 Seasonal Affective Disorder

1. a. depression;   c. anxiety;   e. sensitivity to pain
2. SAD is thought to be caused by *a hormonal problem.*
3. SAD usually affects people who live in places with *cold dark winters.*
4. A common treatment for SAD is *photo-therapy (sitting under special lights).*

7 Advertising slogans

Possible answers:

1. It keeps you slim. / It stops you getting fat.
2. It keeps your skin soft as a baby. / It stops you getting old and wrinkly.
3. They keep your feet warm. / They stop your feet getting cold.

9 Visual dictionary

1. raining   2. snowing   3. foggy   4. cloudy
5. sunny   6. windy   7. stormy   8. icy   9. a flood
10. a blizzard   11. a drought

12 ROMANCE

1 Grammar check

1. arrived; was painting; stopped; went; started; was sitting; was chasing; went; was; rushed; realised; was
2. walked; put up; was going down; was beginning; were cooking; heard; looked up; saw; were running; shouted; looked round

2 Missing words

An English friend *of* mine, Ian, was staying *with* friends *in* America. One night, while he was having a drink *in* a bar, he met an English woman called Jane. They spent a lot *of* time together *during* Ian's holiday and got on very well, but when he left he didn't write down Jane's address *in* England.

Two months later, *in* August, when Ian was relaxing *on* holiday *in* Corfu, he met an Irish woman called Elizabeth. They had a great time together and *at* the end *of* the holiday they exchanged addresses. *By* coincidence, Elizabeth lived very close *to* Ian's parents *in* Manchester, so when he went to visit them *in* October, he decided to call on Elizabeth *at* the same time. He rang the bell to her flat, but when the door opened ...

3 Adjective + noun

dark forest   steep hill   middle-aged couple

romantic scene   amazing coincidence   red rose

nervous smile   surprise party   narrow path

4 What happened and when?

A

1. f   2. g   3. b   4. a   5. c   6. e   7. h   8. d

B

See tapescript on page 135.

5 How many words?

A

1. 6   2. 8   3. 10   4. 10   5. 6   6. 7   7. 8
8. 8

B

These words are all weak forms: the vowel sound is not given its full value in these sentences, and in each case is pronounced /ə/.

1. /ət/   2. /fə/   3. /əv/   4. /wə/   5. /wəz/
6. /əv/   7. /tə/   8. /fə/

6 Love letters

1. false 2. true 3. false 4. false 5. true
6. true 7. false 8. false

7 A poem

See tapescript on page 135 for one possible version of the poem.

13 IT'S BETTER TO TRAVEL THAN TO ARRIVE

1 Verbs and phrases

1. belong 2. hire 3. do 4. take out 5. book
6. run 7. fill in 8. bother 9. checked
10. get/have

2 Before leaving home ...

1. before going
2. after eating
3. before going
4. after missing
5. before going
6. before turning
7. after preparing (or cooking)
8. before looking

3 I want some information

See tapescript on page 135.

4 Sorry to bother you, but ...

Possible answers:
1. Does this belong to you?
2. Could you open your suitcase?
3. Can I have one straightaway?
4. How often do they run?
5. Could you describe it for me?
6. Could you fill in this form, please?
7. How long will it take?
8. Can you deliver it when it arrives?

6 The last minute

	Andrew	Patti
1. Check the windows are locked	✓	✓
2. Turn off the gas	✓	✗
3. Unplug all the electrical appliances	✗	✗
4. Say goodbye to your neighbour	✓	✓
5. Check your passport and tickets	✗	✓
6. Hide all your valuable things	✗	✓
7. Look in the rooms to make sure you haven't forgotten anything	✓	✓
8. Turn off the water	✗	✗
9. Draw the curtains	✗	✓
10. Go to the toilet	✓	✓

7 Lovely to be here

A

Possible answer:

Dear Klaus,

We're on our way to Vienna for a short holiday, and at the moment we're flying over Germany. So far the journey has been fine. The food is quite good and we've just seen *Howard's End* – it's the in-flight movie. We are both feeling a bit tired now, but fortunately we should arrive in about half an hour.

See you in a week's time,

Yours,

Paula and Marco

B

Possible answer:

Dear Klaus,

We've been in Vienna for three days, and we're having a great time. The weather is cold and sunny and we've been to the Vienna Woods several times. Yesterday we went to several museums and art galleries and tomorrow we're going to a famous riding school.

See you in a few days.

Best wishes,

Paula and Marco

PS Tell us if we've made any mistakes.

9 Visual dictionary

1. aircraft landing 2. scales 3. check-in
4. aircraft taking off 5. departure lounge
6. customs officer 7. luggage 8. passport control
9. security check 10. duty-free shop 11. queue
12. left luggage lockers 13. bar

14 POSSESSIONS

1 *For* and *since*

For:

a week; two years; a couple of minutes; over a month; three or four weeks; a century; at least ten days; months and months; a little while; ages.

Since:

six o'clock; last Tuesday; yesterday; the end of June; last November; December 12th; this morning; I wrote to you; mid August; I was 16.

2 Past participles

See tapescript on page 135.

3 Bedside table and bedside lamp

Possible compounds (there are more, but these are the most useful):

coffee bar; coffee beans; coffee break; coffee cup; coffee mill; coffee pot; coffee shop.

book club; bookends; bookseller; bookshelf; bookshop; bookstall.

sports day; sports jacket; sportsman; sportswoman; sportswear; sports field; sports centre; sports shop.

fire alarm; fire brigade; fire drill; fire engine; fire escape; fire extinguisher; fireman; firewoman; firefighter.

eyelash; eyelid; eye-shadow; eyesight.
french bean; french bread; french dressing; french fries; Frenchman; Frenchwoman.

4 Electrical appliances

1. calculator   2. compact disc player
3. microwave oven   4. digital watch
5. video camera   6. clock radio   7. car radio/stereo
8. mobile phone   9. washing machine
10. compact camera   11. computer
12. television with remote control   13. video recorder

5 Problems with electrical appliances

Speaker 1: She loses the guarantee. This is a problem if something goes wrong with the appliance.
Speaker 2: Sometimes there is no plug on the appliance, and he isn't very good at fitting plugs.
Speaker 3: She can't programme her video.
Speaker 4: Bad assembly instructions which the man can't understand.
Speaker 5: He doesn't read the assembly instructions and then he gets things wrong and has to go back to the shop.
Speaker 6: Buying batteries for her camera that are the wrong size.

9 Visual dictionary

1. bathroom   2. roof   3. wardrobe   4. rug
5. chest of drawers   6. chimney   7. shower
8. bath   9. toilet   10. washbasin   11. bedroom
12. double bed   13. bedside table   14. study
15. bookcase   16. computer   17. mobile phone
18. calculator   19. desk
20. lounge (also *living room*)
21. portrait (more general word *picture*)
22. french windows   23. fireplace   24. armchair
25. coffee table   26. hi-fi   27. hall   28. path

15 RULES

1 Places

The Canary Islands; Mount Everest; Lake Constance; The Atlantic Ocean; The Black Sea; The National Gallery; The Atlas Mountains; The River Nile.

2 Obligation and permission

Possible answers:
1. We had to book a room.
2. We couldn't stay less than two nights / stay only one night.
3. We had to use the car park at the back / park in the street.
4. We couldn't eat in our room / have meals in our room.
5. Men had to wear shirts and ties in the dining room.
6. When we left, we couldn't stay in the room after 10.30 am.
7. We had to pay in cash / by cheque.

3 Don't make a mistake

A

wait one's turn; kick a ball; leave the room; address a letter; wear a uniform; blow one's nose; shake hands; make a call; break a rule; take an exam.

B

1. shake   2. leave   3. wear   4. wait
5. blow   6. kick   7. take   8. address
9. make   10. break

4 Right or wrong?

See tapescript for Exercise 5 on page 136.

16 KEEPING THE CUSTOMER SATISFIED

1 If it rains ...

A

1. i   2. d   3. j   4. c   5. a   6. g   7. b   8. e
9. f   10. h

B

Possible answers:
3. If the bank is open, I'll deposit the money.
4. If she doesn't speak very quickly, I'll be able to understand her.
5. If I pass the exam, I'll be delighted.
6. If I don't see Catherine, I'll phone her this evening.
7. If I don't get lost, I'll be back very soon.
8. If I don't miss the bus, I'll be there by six.
9. If the music isn't very loud, it'll be OK.
10. If I don't win lots of money, I won't be able to afford a holiday.

2 Forming opposites

unhelpful; unfriendly; inefficient; impolite; unreliable; illegal; unemployed; impossible; inexperienced; illogical; unnecessary; unsuitable.

3 Syllables and word stress

A

Two syllables: message; Wednesday; research; polite; business
Three syllables: opposite; questionnaire; appearance; suitable
Four syllables: experience; reliable; economist; competition
Five syllables: vegetarian

B

1st syllable	2nd syllable	3rd syllable
client	employer	education
opposite	experience	questionnaire
message	research	competition
Wednesday	reliable	vegetarian
business	economist	
suitable	polite	
	appearance	

4 Synonyms and opposites in business

1. employees
2. gone up/risen
3. reliable
4. clients
5. take out
6. sold
7. loss
8. fallen / gone down / decreased
9. unreliable
10. lose; increase / put up / raise

5 Nouns formed with -ness

The three adjectives which do not form nouns with *-ness* are: efficient (efficiency); warm (warmth); stupid (stupidity).

The others are: politeness; happiness; illness; madness; weakness; rudeness; sickness; blindness; sadness; loneliness; kindness; helpfulness.

7 What does she think?

1. **population:** She thinks it might rise.
2. a. **life expectancy for women:** She thinks it will rise.
   b. **life expectancy for men:** It probably won't rise.
3. **age of retirement:** She doesn't think it will change for women, but it might come down to 60 for men.
4. **diet:** She thinks it will change and we will eat less meat and fats and more fruit and vegetables.
5. **money we spend on clothes:** We will spend a bit more.
6. **shops:** She thinks more shops will be located outside of towns and people might shop from home more.
7. **leisure:** People will watch more TV.
8. **foreign travel:** People will definitely travel more.
9. **eating out:** She thinks people will eat out more.

8 Business letters

Model answer:

> *3 Acacia Avenue*
> *London N5*
>
> *The Manager*
> *Sunland Furnishings*
> *East Street*
> *Sunleigh*
> *Essex*
>
> *28 May 1995*
>
> *Dear Sir*
>
> *I am interested in your new 'Summer Shade' range of garden furniture, and I would be grateful if you could send me a copy of your current brochure and price list.*
>
> *I look forward to hearing from you.*
>
> *Yours faithfully*
>
> *John Patterson*

17 PICTURE THIS!

1 Logical endings

Possible answers:

1. I bought a dictionary so that I could look up new words.
2. He does a lot of overtime so that he can earn more/extra money.
3. She got up early so that she had time for a big breakfast.
4. I always go to the supermarket on Friday so that I don't have to go at the weekend.
5. We must go now, otherwise we'll be late.
6. Take an umbrella, otherwise you'll get wet.
7. She must work hard, otherwise she might fail the exam.
8. Write down new words in your notebook, otherwise you might forget them.

2 Put them in order

1. First of all, try to learn a few words in our language.
2. Secondly, make sure you buy a good guide book.
3. Thirdly, try to avoid the usual tourist places.
4. Finally, don't forget to phone me when you arrive.

3 Word partnerships

A

make: a mistake; an appointment; a noise.
do: the shopping; someone a favour; homework.
tell: a story; the truth; a lie.
take: a photo; a taxi; a shower.

B

1. make
2. tell
3. take
4. tell
5. make
6. make
7. tell
8. do

C

1. careless
2. honest
3. lazy
4. dishonest
5. unreliable
6. irritating
7. funny
8. mean

4 Wordsearch

5 Photo in St James Park

See tapescript on page 137.

8 Visual dictionary

1. sea   2. yacht   3. clouds   4. rocks   5. beach
6. traffic lights   7. motor cycle   8. lorry
9. postbox   10. pedestrian crossing   11. pedestrians
12. field   13. tractor   14. sheep   15. gate
16. fence

18 LISTS

1 Could you lend me some money?

A

1. an invitation   2. a suggestion   3. a request
4. advice   5. an apology   6. thanks   7. a plan
8. an excuse

B

See tapescript on page 137.

2 On the telephone

1. A: Hello?
    B: Is that John?
    A: Yes. (*Yes, speaking* is possible here but a bit formal.)
    B: Oh, hello, John. It's Hans. (*This is Hans* is also
        possible.)

2. A: Good morning, Reebok.
    B: Good morning. I want to speak to Mr Graham,
        please. (in American English *speak with*.)
    A: Yes, who's calling, please?
    B: My name is Maria Selbeck.
    A: Right, one moment. I'll put you through.

3. A: Hello?
    B: Oh, I'd like to speak to Jasna, please.
    A: I'm sorry, she's out. Can I take a message?
    B: No, it's OK. I'll ring back later.

4. A: Hello?
    B: Oh, hello, Catherine; it's Brian. How are you?
    A: Fine, thanks. And you?
    B: Yes, I'm fine too.

3 Lexical sets

A

Answers on recording:
1. fork   2. blouse   3. leather   4. medium
5. full board   6. main course   7. cigars
8. washbasin   9. silver   10. diamonds

5 Complete the phrase

1. afraid not   2. think so
3. Never mind (*or* That's OK *or* Don't worry)
4. apart from (*or* except for)   5. on his own
6. on foot   7. at least
8. How about (*or* What about)
9. that's very kind of you   10. Fine, thanks

6 Memory aids

Suggested answers:
a. 1, 8   b. 13   c. 6   d. 3, 7, possibly 12
e. 7, 12   f. 1

7 A list of facts

The list shows the time taken over the centuries to go
round the world.

Date	Craft	Time
1519–21	*Vittoria* (sailing ship)	2 years
1960	USS *Triton* (nuclear submarine)	2 months and 25 days
1929	*Graf Zeppelin* (airship)	21 days 7 hours and 34 minutes
1924	*Chicago* (aircraft)	14 days 15 hours and 11 minutes
1957	USAF Boeing B–52	1 day 21 hours and 19 minutes
1967	*Cosmos 169* (satellite)	80 minutes and 30.6 seconds

8 Language learning

Possible answers:

I often make lists because when I write down words in
my notebook, it helps me to remember them. And I can
refer to them again in the future.

I never make lists because I am a bit lazy, but also
because it doesn't help me to learn new vocabulary very
effectively. I prefer to say the words over and over again.

I keep a record of vocabulary in this way: I organise
most words into topics and keep a page for each one.
When I learn new words about a topic I can add them
to the page.

I translate words into my own language when there is a
simple translation, and when I cannot write a definition
for a word in English.

I prefer a monolingual dictionary because it helps me to
think in English and gives me reading practice. I don't
trust my bilingual dictionary.

I prefer a bilingual dictionary because it's much easier
and quicker to use than a monolingual dictionary.
Sometimes I can't understand the definitions when they
are written in English because they use words I don't
know.

Working with my speaking partner is good for my
English. It was difficult at first but it really gives me a lot
of speaking practice outside of class. Now I feel quite
relaxed about speaking English.

Speaking on the telephone in English is very difficult
because you can't use your hands to express ideas and
sometimes it is difficult because voices are not so clear
on the phone.

10 Visual dictionary

1. spoon   2. fork   3. knife   4. cigar   5. cigarette
6. pipe   7. ring   8. earrings   9. bracelet
10. tennis racket   11. ball   12. trainers   13. shorts
14. sink   15. washing machine   16. fridge
17. (four of) clubs   18. (seven of) diamonds
19. (ten of) spades   20. (six of) hearts   21. hammer
22. screwdriver   23. saw   24. corkscrew
25. bottle opener   26. tin/can opener

19 PUT YOUR TRUST IN OTHERS

1 Correct the mistakes
1. What will you do if it **rains** tomorrow?
2. correct.
3. If he **lost** his job, it would be terrible for the family.
4. We **wouldn't know** what to say if she refused to help us this evening.
5. **We'll** have a great time if you come to the restaurant with us.
6. correct.
7. correct.
8. If somebody **broke** into your flat tonight, what would you do?
   or If somebody breaks into your flat tonight, what **will** you do?
9. If she **gets** the job, we'll be delighted.
10. I would **complain** if a restaurant served me bad food.

2 Just imagine
1. If I didn't live near the centre, I'd need a car.
2. If I worked on Saturdays, I wouldn't go to bed very late on Fridays.
   or If I worked on Saturdays, I'd go to bed early on Fridays.
3. If I didn't have a big dog, I wouldn't get lots of / much exercise.
4. If I ate at home often, I would need a dishwasher.
5. If I drank coffee at night, it would keep me awake.
6. If I understood the financial pages, I would read them.
7. If the tickets weren't so expensive / were cheaper, we would go.
8. If we didn't have a babysitter, we wouldn't be able to go out.

3 From verb to noun
A
Nouns:
explanation; refusal; acceptance; belief; invitation; complaint; offer; agreement.
B
1. invitation   2. refused   3. complaint
4. explanation   5. offered   6. believe   7. accept
8. agreement

4 I'm very boring!
1. bored   2. depressing   3. embarrassing
4. surprised   5. disgusting   6. shocked
7. interested   8. frightened   9. boring
10. depressed

6 Lexical connections
1. i   2. a   3. b   4. j   5. g   6. c   7. h   8. f
9. e   10. d

8 Conditional sentences
Possible answers:
A
If I didn't have a car, I would walk a lot more.
If I didn't have a car, I would go to work by bus.
If I didn't have a car, I wouldn't be able to visit my friends so much.

If I had a car, it would be very convenient.
If I had a car, I would drive into the country every weekend.
If I had a car, I wouldn't need to use the bus so much.
B
If I weren't married, I would probably go out a lot more.
If I weren't married, I might be lonely some of the time.
If I weren't married, I would still live with my parents.

If I were married, I wouldn't live with my parents.
If I were married, I might have different interests.
If I were married, I wouldn't see my friends so much.
C
If I didn't have a job, I wouldn't have much money.
If I didn't have a job, I would be very unhappy.
If I didn't have a job, I would have nothing to do all day.

If I had a job, I would have more money to spend.
If I had a job, I might feel quite different.
If I had a job, I would have less free time.

20 THE SENSES

1 Agreeing
1. Neither can I.   6. So am I.
2. So do I.   7. Neither am I.
3. Neither do I.   8. Neither can I.
4. So can I.   9. So do I.
5. So do I.   10. So am I.

2 Find the first letter
1. I'm not sure but I think it might rain again tonight.
2. Do you think there will be people living on the moon in twenty years' time?
3. She's sure she won't pass her exams because she hasn't worked hard enough.
4. The doctor thinks he'll recover quickly from the operation.
5. I don't think our teacher will be annoyed if we forget to do our homework.
6. I'm absolutely certain my sister will be late. She always is.

3 Compound words
A
chewing gum; doorbell; computer keyboard; after-shave; furniture polish; boiled egg; paint brush; soap powder; digital watch
B
1. paint brush   2. digital watch   3. chewing gum
4. boiled egg   5. soap powder   6. furniture polish
7. after-shave   8. computer keyboard   9. doorbell

4 Listen and answer

See tapescript on page 137.

5 Odd one out

1. banana (/ɑː/; all the other words have /eɪ/.)
2. nylon (/ɒ/; all the other words have /ʌ/.)
3. speak (/iː/; all the other words have /e/.)
4. orange (/ɪ/; all the other words have /æ/.)
5. smoke (/əʊ/; all the other words have /ɒ/.)
6. Norway (/ɔː/; all the other words have /ɜː/.)

6 Setting the scene

He can see people's teeth.
He can see people smoking and drinking.
He can taste Scotch (whisky).
He can smell smoke.
He can feel the bar-rail behind his shoulders.

Possible answers:
He can probably hear laughter, people shouting, music
    and the sound of glass.
He can probably smell food, perfume and drinks
    prepared by the barman.
He can probably see people pushing, lighting cigarettes,
    picking up and putting down drinks, and dancing.

9 Visual dictionary

wall   paintbrush   paint   earring   jeans   jacket
tin of paint   fireplace   marble   polish   cloth
ashtray   cigar   cigar smoke   digital watch
armchair   cushion   cat   fur   basket
washing powder   chewing gum   garlic   desk
perfume   lemons   oranges   grapes   bowl of fruit

21 TIME

1 Past versus present

Possible answers:
1. I'm retired now, but I used to work in a bank.
2. I've got contact lenses now, but I used to wear glasses.
3. I go jogging every day, so I'm quite fit, but I used to
    be very unhealthy/unfit.
4. I think I'm quite self-confident now, but I used to be
    shy.
5. I get on very well with my sister now, but we used to
    have fights.
6. Car engines are very complicated these days, but they
    used to be simple.
7. I really like studying English now, but I used to hate
    it.
8. I spend a lot of time at home these days, but I used to
    go out a lot.

2 Mental gymnastics

1. 892   2. 90   3. 334   4. 1938   5. 1490
6. 1st January 2000   7. 1628   8. 12

3 *Saw* or *have seen*?

3. I saw her last night.
4. I haven't seen her since Tuesday.
5. I saw her in August.
6. I saw her yesterday.
7. I haven't seen her in the last three weeks.
8. I haven't seen her yet.
9. I saw her before you came in.
10. I saw her at six o'clock.
11. I haven't seen her this month.
12. I saw her when I was in Rome.
13. I haven't seen her since I arrived.
14. I saw her ten years ago.
15. I haven't seen her since last year.

4 At three o'clock in the morning

Woman	Man
1. at 12.15 in 1960.	at about 9.30 in the morning on a Friday in 1957.
2. in October.	in September when I was four and a half.
3. in August, perhaps July.	in the summer.
4. in the morning.	at night and in the morning.
5. at around 9.30, 10.	at 9 o'clock.
6. at night.	in the afternoon, not so much at night.
7. in winter.	on a Sunday.
8. so long ago I can't remember.	a class that I did in November.
9. every night.	at night.
10. on Christmas Day.	on the first of May.

5 Contextual guesswork

scheme: plan/idea
adopt: use
reckons: believes/thinks
backed: supported
hardly: almost not

8 Messages

Possible answers:
1. John rang while you were out. Could you ring him
    before he leaves the office at 6.00? He wants to meet
    you for dinner tonight.
2. Mr Bassett wants you to contact him when you are
    free, because he needs to arrange a meeting with you.
3. Maria says she won't be back until 10.00, so she's
    sorry but she can't meet you this evening after all.
4. A parcel arrived for you this morning. Can you come
    and collect it whenever you are free? It looks very
    exciting.
5. Your mother phoned while you were at the dentist.
    She said she needed to speak to you sometime today.
6. Phone the hospital as soon as possible. It's about your
    next-door neighbour. Don't worry; it's nothing
    serious.

22 A SENSE OF HISTORY

1 He was arrested outside the bank

A

past passive
future passive
present passive
past passive
present passive
future passive

B

1. was taken; was given
2. was written; was published; will be translated
3. are made; are exported; are sold
4. was made; was directed; will be shown
5. was designed; was built; are *or* were buried

2 Lexical sets

Possible answers:

RANKS/TITLES: a general; prime minister; politician; captain; president; emperor.
WAR: fight; enemy; win; lose; shoot; war.
HOSPITAL: ambulance; antibiotics; doctor; cure; treat; accident; hospital.

3 More horrible history

1. who; which; Although
2. who; However; which; Although

4 From verb to noun

Verb	Noun	Verb	Noun
die	death	elect	election
murder	murder	explode	explosion
escape	escape	develop	development
invade	invasion	assassinate	assassination
win	win	invent	invention
resign	resignation	destroy	destruction

Note: There are other possible answers – murderer, assassin, escapee, etc.

5 Word stress

die	death	elect	election
murder	murder	explode	explosion
escape	escape	develop	development
invade	invasion	assassinate	assassination
win	win	invent	invention
resign	resignation	destroy	destruction

6 The fate of the Russian royal family – fact or fiction?

B

1. True   2. False   3. True   4. True   5. False
6. False   7. False

7 Dictation

A

See tapescript on page 138.

B

1. The fire which destroyed the building started in one of the bedrooms.
2. The man who saw the thief lives on the other side of the street.
3. The accident which was on the front page of the newspaper happened near our house.
4. The boy who used to steal my apples later became a policeman.

23 WHOSE LIFE IS IT ANYWAY?

1 What do you call them?

B

	Joumana	Stefan
1. your friends	by their first names	by their first names
2. your doctor	by his title	by his title
3. your teacher	Mary	Mr Curran
4. your boss	by his first name	by his surname
5. your landlord or landlady	by her surname	by his first name
6. your dentist	Mrs Patterson	by his title
7. a stranger in the street	nothing	nothing
8. your tax inspector	nothing	nothing
9. a waiter in a restaurant	nothing	'Excuse me, please'
10. your grandparents	Gran and Grandpa	Grandma and Grandpa
11. your newspaper seller	Arun	nothing
12. your bank manager	by her surname	Mrs Wetherall
13. your parents	Mum and Dad	Ma and Pa

C

In Britain, these would be the normal answers:

2. Dear Mr/Mrs/Miss/Ms Brown/Gonzalez, etc. or Dear Joan/Pete if you know them well.
3. Dear Mr/Mrs/Miss/Ms Johnston.
4. Dear Mr/Mrs/Miss/Ms Lewis or Dear Sir/Madam.
5. Dear Mr/Mrs/Miss/Ms Arthur or Dear Christine/Alex if you know them well.

2 Careful(ly)

1. hard   2. peacefully   3. peaceful   4. patiently
5. nervous   6. beautifully, terrible   7. quietly
8. dangerously   9. slowly   10. fast, easily
11. careful   12. efficient

3 Politics and religion

A

1. Yes, it's a religious problem.
2. Yes, it's an educational problem.
3. Yes, it's a political problem.
4. Yes, it's a cultural problem.
5. Yes, it's a social problem.

B

6. You must make a choice.
7. Can we make a comparison?
8. Are they getting a divorce?
9. Can you give me some advice?
10. What are your beliefs?

4 Sounds and spelling

choose	/tʃuːz/	unusual	/ʌnjuːʒuəl/
such	/sʌtʃ/	culture	/kʌltʃə/
spider	/spaɪdə/	rhyme	/raɪm/
brain	/breɪn/	strange	/streɪndʒ/
joke	/dʒəʊk/	so	/səʊ/
common	/kɒmən/	politics	/pɒlɪtɪks/
call	/kɔːl/	report	/rɪpɔːt/
surname	/sɜːneɪm/	prefer	/prɪfɜː/

24 CINEMA AND THE ARTS

1 Test your knowledge

Shakespeare wrote *Macbeth*.
Duke Ellington played (the) piano.
War and Peace was written by Tolstoy.
Gabriel García Márquez wrote *100 Years of Solitude*.
The Marriage of Figaro was composed/written by Mozart.
The Pompidou Centre was designed by Richard Rogers.
Guernica was painted by Pablo Picasso.
Elizabeth Taylor was married to Richard Burton.
Psycho was directed by Hitchcock.
The Beatles sang *Eleanor Rigby*.
Akira Kurosawa directed *The Seven Samurai*.
Herbert von Karajan conducted the Berlin Philharmonic
    Orchestra.

2 Theatre and cinema

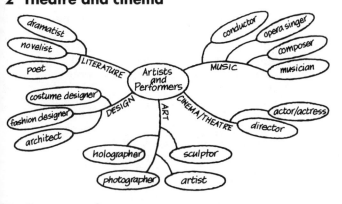

3 Crossword

Across:

1. honest   5. met   7. review   9. ballerina
10. cash   11. tear   14. Goya   15 and 21. sub titles
17. organ   19. once

Down:

1. hardback   2. novelist   3. Steven   4. be
6. theatre   8. cinema   12. solo   13. funny
16. Lake   18. rat   20. ET

4 First names in English

Names that have the sound /iː/:
Sheila, Stephen, Jean, Leo, Neil

Names that have the sound /uː/:
Andrew, Stewart, Julia, Judy

Names that have the sound /ɔː/:
Paul, Lorna, George, Laura

Names that have the sound /əʊ/:
Joan, Rose

Men:
Andrew, Stewart, Paul, George, Stephen, Leo, Neil
Women:
Joan, Rose, Julia, Judy, Lorna, Laura, Sheila, Jean

Famous examples:
Andrew Lloyd Webber, Prince Andrew, Joan Collins,
Joan of Arc, George Bush, Paul McCartney, Neil
Armstrong, Stewart Grainger, Jean Simmons, Neil
Simon.

5 The artistic process

1. Carlo Maria Giulini
2. Woody Allen
3. Stephen King
4. Mitsuko Uchida

6 Playing in a band

A

1. Broken Glass
2. 4
3. 5 years ago
4. piano and keyboards
5. rock
6. pubs and private parties
7. 4
8. Robin

B

1. What's the band called?
2. How many people are (there) in the band?
3. When was the band formed?
4. What (instrument) does Spencer play?
5. What kind of music do they play?
6. Where do they perform?
7. How often do they practise?
8. Who writes most of the music?

9 Visual dictionary

1. guitar   2. drums   3. violin   4. cello
5. saxophone   6. trumpet   7. clarinet   8. flute
9. piano   10. organ   11. curtain   12. stage
13. rows   14. aisle   15. audience

IRREGULAR VERBS AND PHONETIC SYMBOLS

Irregular verbs

Infinitive	Past simple	Past participle
be	was/were	been
become	became	become
begin	began	begun
bend	bent	bent
bite	bit	bitten
blow	blew	blown
break	broke	broken
bring	brought	brought
build	built	built
buy	bought	bought
can	could	(been able)
catch	caught	caught
choose	chose	chosen
come	came	come
cost	cost	cost
cut	cut	cut
do	did	done
draw	drew	drawn
dream	dreamt	dreamt
drink	drank	drunk
drive	drove	driven
eat	ate	eaten
fall	fell	fallen
feel	felt	felt
fight	fought	fought
find	found	found
fly	flew	flown
forget	forgot	forgotten
get	got	got
give	gave	given
go	went	gone (been)
have	had	had
hear	heard	heard
hit	hit	hit
hold	held	held
hurt	hurt	hurt
keep	kept	kept
know	knew	known
learn	learnt	learnt
leave	left	left
lend	lent	lent
let	let	let
lie	lay	lain
lose	lost	lost
make	made	made
mean	meant	meant
meet	met	met
pay	paid	paid
put	put	put
read /riːd/	read /red/	read /red/
ride	rode	ridden
ring	rang	rung
rise	rose	risen
run	ran	run
say	said	said
see	saw	seen
sell	sold	sold

Infinitive	Past simple	Past participle
send	sent	sent
set	set	set
shake	shook	shaken
shine	shone	shone
shoot	shot	shot
show	showed	shown
shut	shut	shut
sing	sang	sung
sit	sat	sat
sleep	slept	slept
speak	spoke	spoken
spell	spelt	spelt
spend	spent	spent
stand	stood	stood
steal	stole	stolen
swim	swam	swum
take	took	taken
teach	taught	taught
tell	told	told
think	thought	thought
throw	threw	thrown
understand	understood	understood
wake	woke	woken
wear	wore	worn
win	won	won
write	wrote	written

Phonetic symbols

Vowels

Symbol	Example
/iː/	see
/i/	happy
/ɪ/	big
/e/	bed
/æ/	sad
/ʌ/	sun
/ɑː/	car
/ɒ/	pot
/ɔː/	taught
/ʊ/	pull
/uː/	boot
/ɜː/	bird
/ə/	among
	produce
/eɪ/	date
/aɪ/	time
/ɔɪ/	boy
/əʊ/	note
/aʊ/	town
/ɪə/	ear
/eə/	there
/ʊə/	tour

Consonants

Symbol	Example
/b/	back
/d/	dog
/ð/	then
/dʒ/	joke
/f/	far
/g/	go
/h/	hot
/j/	young
/k/	key
/l/	learn
/m/	make
/n/	note
/ŋ/	sing
/p/	pan
/r/	ran
/s/	soon
/ʃ/	fish
/t/	top
/tʃ/	chart
/θ/	thin
/v/	view
/w/	went
/z/	zone
/ʒ/	pleasure

Stress

Stress is indicated by a small box above the stressed syllable.
Example: advertisement

ACKNOWLEDGEMENTS

Authors' acknowledgements

We must first thank our fellow authors Joanne Collie and Stephen Slater. Their creativity and ideas have been a great source of inspiration to us.

We are also indebted to Gillian Lazar for her detailed and invaluable comments on the final manuscript. For the same reason, our thanks to other readers who commented on all or part of the manuscript: Diann Gruber, Sue Garvin, Virginia Garcia, Carol Hermann, Anthony Nicholson and Antonio Marcelino Campo.

For the piloting we must also thank James Dingle, who edited the pilot edition and coordinated this stage of the project.

Friends and colleagues have given us permission to use their ideas and activities – or in some cases just inspired us. We would like to thank Philip Dale, Petrina Cliff, Guilherme Pacheco, Tom Bradbury, Alastair and Toshi Banton, Pat Lane and Roz Canning. And a big thank you to the staff of International House and the London School of English for their continued support and encouragement.

At Cambridge University Press, Kate Boyce has been magnificent in guiding the project through the complex stages of editing and production; without her it would never have happened. We would also like to thank Helena Gomm for her astonishing efficiency and good humour in editing the book; and Randell Harris for his stylish and original design. And then thanks to the producer of all the recorded material, Martin Williamson, and the staff at AVP.

Finally, our thanks go to our commissioning editor, Peter Donovan, who set the whole thing in motion, and to the rest of the staff at Cambridge University Press.

The authors and publishers would like to thank the following institutions and teachers for their help in testing the material and for the invaluable feedback which they provided:

University of Canberra TESOL Centre, Belconnen, Australia; Queensland College of English, Brisbane, Australia; Waratah Education Centre, Manly, Australia; Insearch Language Centre, UTS, Sydney, Australia; Centro Linguistico di Ateneo, Parma University, Parma, Italy; International House, Turin, Italy; The Cambridge School, Verona, Italy; Languages International, Auckland, New Zealand; Cambridge English Studies, La Coruña, Spain; Dilko English, Istanbul, Turkey; Chichester School of English, Chichester, UK; Regent Hove, Hove, UK; Newcastle College, Newcastle, UK.

The authors and publishers are grateful to the following copyright holders for permission to reproduce copyright material. While every endeavour has been made, it has not been possible to identify the sources of all material used and in such cases the publishers would welcome information from copyright sources. Apologies are expressed for any omissions.

p. 6: adapted extract from *Dark Angel* by Sally Beauman published by Bantam Books, reprinted by permission of Peters Fraser & Dunlop Group Ltd; p. 7: material about Russell Hoban by permission of David Higham Associates and about Jessie Kesson by permission of John Johnson Limited taken from the BBC's *The Late Show*; p. 12: jokes from *Groans* by Sylvana Nown published by Futura, reprinted by permission of Little, Brown; p. 16: adapted extract from *The History of Topographical Maps: Symbols, Pictures and Surveys* by P D A Harvey, published by Thames and Hudson Ltd, London; pp. 20, 21: extract from *Drawing on the Right Side of the Brain* by Betty Edwards, published by Souvenir Press Ltd; pp. 24, 25: adapted material from *New Scientist* (December 24/31 1988) © *New Scientist*; p. 29: material and visuals adapted from *Juggling for All* by Colin Francome and Charlie Holland, published by David & Charles, 1987, reprinted by permission of Colin Francome; p.30: 'Who'd be a juggler' by Cicely Herbert from *The Kingfisher Book of Children's Poetry* edited by Michael Rosen, published by Kingfisher, 1985, reprinted by permission of Cicely Herbert; p. 34: extract from *Handwriting Analysis: The Complete Basic Book* by Karen Amend and Mary Ruiz, published by Newcastle Publishing Co, USA; p. 39: adapted extracts from the *Time Out London Shopping Guide*, compiled by Lindsey Bareham, reprinted by permission of Time Out Magazine Ltd; p. 43: extract from *Japan – a travel survival kit* by Ian L McQueen, reprinted by permission of Ian L McQueen; extract from *Colombia – a travel survival kit* by Krzsytof Dydynski (1988), reprinted by permission of Lonely Planet Publications; extracts from *Rough Guide to Brittany & Normandy* by Greg Ward, 1987, and *Rough Guide to Amsterdam* by Martin Dunford and Jack Holland, published by Rough Guides Ltd © Rough Guides; p.54: extract from *Discovering the Weather* by P Wright, reproduced by permission of Longman Group UK; p. 55: adapted text based on information from *Practical Health* magazine; p. 60: letter by Evelyn Waugh to Laura Herbert, 4 August 1936, from *The Letters of Evelyn Waugh*, edited by Mark Amory, published by Weidenfeld & Nicolson, reprinted by permission of Weidenfeld & Nicolson and Peters Fraser & Dunlop; letter by Rupert Brooke to Cathleen Nesbitt, 31 May 1913, from *The Letters of Rupert Brooke* edited by Geoffrey Keynes, reprinted by permission of Faber and Faber Limited; p. 61: 'Why I didn't get you a valentine's card' from *Glad to wear glasses* by John Hegley, reprinted by permission of Andre Deutsch Ltd, 1990; p. 64: extract from 'Orf one goes again' reprinted by permission of Gwen Robyns, 1988; p. 69: extract from 'Why you can't set your video' by William Mullen © Copyrighted February 11, 1990, Chicago Tribune Company. All rights reserved. Used with permission; p. 78: extract adapted from *Woman* magazine; p. 83: 'Photo in St James' Park from *Glad to wear glasses* by John Hegley, reprinted by permission of Andre Deutsch Ltd, 1990; p. 87: extract from *Your Memory – a user's guide* by Alan Baddeley, published by Penguin Books, compilation copyright © Multimedia Books Ltd 1993; p. 88: extract from *The Big Book of Facts, Records and Lists* by Elizabeth Holt © Elizabeth Holt, reproduced with permission from Pan Macmillan Children's Books; p. 92: extract from *The Education Guardian*, 3/9/91; p. 97: extract from 'The Great Switcheroo' in *Switch Bitch* by Roald Dahl published by Penguin Books, reprinted by permission of Alfred A Knopf Inc.; p. 97: extract based on *Once Upon A Time* by Mario Rinvolucri published by Cambridge University Press; p. 101: extract from '25-hour clocks' by Fiona Mooney © Daily Mail/Solo; p. 102: 'The clock on the wall' by Samih Al-Qasim from *Victims of a Map*, reprinted by permission of Saqi Books; 'Everything Changes' from *100 Poems on the Underground* edited by Gerard Benson, Judith Chernaik and Cicely Herbert, reprinted by permission of Cicely Herbert; extract from *Turn, Turn, Turn* by Pete Seeger © 1962 Melody Trails Inc., New York, N.Y. Assigned to TRO Essex Music Ltd. London SW10 0SZ. International Copyright Secured. Used by permission. All rights reserved; p. 105: texts adapted from *Horrible History* by Tim Wood and Ian Dicks © Simon & Schuster Young Books, reproduced by permission of Simon & Schuster Young Books, Hemel Hempstead, UK; p. 111: extracts from *Choose Your Baby's Name* by Rosalind Ferguson published by Penguin Books, 1987 © Rosalind Ferguson and Market House, 1987, reproduced by permission of Penguin Books Ltd; p. 116: Woody Allen extract by David Remnick reprinted by permission of *Saturday Review*.

The authors and publishers are grateful to the following illustrators and photographic sources:

Illustrators: Veronica Bailey: p. 67; Kathy Baxendale: pp. 11, 15, 29, 106; ; Paul Dickinson: pp. 37, 63; Daren Diss: p. 92; David Downton: p. 55; Richard Eckford: pp. 23, 99; Max Ellis: pp. 30, 109; Philip Emms: pp. 12, 46, 85; Martin Fish: pp 64, 76; Spike Gerrell: p. 95; Sue Hillward-Harris: pp. 58, 90; Terry Kennett: p. 72; Joanna Kerr: pp. 22, 32, 68, 87; Vicky Lowe: p. 42; Amanda MacPhail: pp. 119–131; Pete Neame: pp. 24, 74, 105; Tracy Rich: pp. 41, 101; David Williams: pp. 21 *b*, 27, 59; Celia Witchard: pp. 39, 57.

Photographic sources: Barnaby's Picture Library: pp. 39 (photo Gill Hahessy) and 81 *l*; The British Museum: p. 16 *t*; Camera Press: pp. 11 (Paul Steinemann), 71 *r* (Hilary McLaughlin), 116 *bl* (Jane Bown) and 116 *br* (Bob Penn); J. Allen Cash Photo Library: p. 81 *r*; John Cleare Mountain Camera: p. 71 *l*; Gronlands Nationalmuseum, Greenland: p. 16 *b*; Geoff Howard: p. 5; Hulton Deutsch Collection: p. 60 *bl*; Image Bank: p. 4 (David Vance); Kobal Collection: p. 116 *tl*; Performing Arts Library: p. 116 *tr* (Clive Barda); Popperfoto: p. 106; Thames and Hudson Ltd, London: p. 16 *l* and *r*, maps from *The History of Topographical Maps: Symbols, Pictures and Surveys* by P D A Harvey; Topham Picturepoint: pp. 7 *t* and 60 *tr*; Virago Press: p. 7 *b*.

t = top, *b* = bottom, *c* = centre, *l* = left, *r* = right

Design by Newton Harris
Picture research by Marilyn Rawlings

The authors and publishers are grateful to the following for permission to reproduce photographs on the cover:

Image Bank: *l* (Larry Dale Gordon) and *r* (Kim Steele); Tony Stone Images: *tc* (Rainer Grosskopf), *bc* (Donald Nausbaum) and inset right (Frank Cezus).